Standard
1984
U.S. COIN
Catalogue

- BUY AND SELL PRICES
- Scott catalogue numbers
- Mint records from 1793 to date
- Check list and grading guide
- Fully illustrated

BARNES & NOBLE BOOKS
A DIVISION OF HARPER & ROW, PUBLISHERS
New York, Cambridge, Philadelphia, San Francisco
London, Mexico City, São Paulo, Sydney

CONTENTS

Introduction and editorial collaboration by Joseph H. Rose, President, Harmer Rooke Numismatists Ltd., 3 East 57th St., New York, N.Y. 10022. Pricing editor, Harry Miller, President, Millers' Mint Ltd., 313 E. Main St., Patchogue, N.Y. 11772.

First BARNES & NOBLE BOOKS edition published 1983.

LIBRARY OF CONGRESS CATALOG CARD NUMBER 75-4143

ISBN: 0-06-465151-7

INTRODUCTION

Whether you are a novice coin collector or an experienced numismatist, this book will serve as a guide to you in the buying and selling of coins. The price lists contained herein may fluctuate at different times, but the prices are given as a guide to help you in your understanding of general numismatic values in the coin market.

The price of coins has risen for various reasons: people who buy coins as an investment feel this is a way to hedge inflation; they consider that the loss of the dollar's purchasing power will be countered by the higher value of the coins as their prices increase, and as time goes by.

Also, speculators in the metal market buy gold and silver coins, not to collect them, but to melt them down and convert the metal into bullion. The bullion is then offered for sale in the metal markets all over the world. Especially in the case of gold, the price has gone very high as a reflection of monetary crises not only in the United States but in other countries too.

These conditions tend to drive up the prices of collectors' coins, so that those who pursue this fascinating hobby must be selective and careful in buying specimens to add to a collection. Thus, the information and pricing list provided by this book will prove invaluable as a sound guide in the acquisition or disposition of numismatic items on the open market.

In addition to price guides, herein is contained information about the economics and history of coinage, which adds to the fascination of coin collecting as a hobby.

GOLD
AS A METAL AND IN COINS

Throughout history, gold has held a fascination for all mankind. Not only has it been the backing for the currency of virtually all the nations of the world but it has also been the basis by which most foreign trade is consummated. While much gold still remains below ground waiting to be mined, there is not enough above ground to satisfy the financial needs of the ever-increasing international trade. Therefore, to facilitate these transactions, paper money, really governmental promissory notes, has come to be an acceptable medium of exchange, even though today it is only partly backed by gold reserves. It is trust in the issuing government that leads to the ready acceptance of paper currency.

But the demand for gold remains, and thus the fixed price of $35 per ounce set by the US in 1933 has no credence on the market. Rather, the price is set by supply and demand, as with every other commodity. So it is that the current world inflationary cycle has caused the price of gold to rise higher and higher, today hovering near the $600 per ounce level.

Prices of gold coins have soared because of this and the ensuing rise in demand. Purchasers of such coins are well advised to select and buy gold (or any) coins only from dealers who have sound reputations in the numismatic field.

SILVER
AS A METAL AND IN COINS

Almost from the inception of coinage nearly 3000 years ago, silver has been one of the three metals most widely used for money, the others being gold (or electrum) and bronze (or copper). In the beginning, and almost to present times, the intrinsic value of a coin was intended to represent its exact value if melted down. (In other words, a silver dollar contained a dollar's worth of silver). It is interesting to note, however that in times of stress-war, economic problems, etc. precious metals tend to disappear from circulation as people hoard against the uncertain future. Such has been the history of silver. Due to unsettled times, increased use for industry, and the inflationary cycle, it became more and more impractical for governments to mint coins of silver. By 1964 the intrinsic value of the metal had made the coins worth more than their face value, and so the practice of making coins of silver disappeared completely, all over the world. Today, only some commemoratives and special issues are made of silver, and these usually have high face values to pay for the intrinsic worth.

Most governments are now engaged in melting down previous silver issues to replace dwindling stockpiles of the precious metal. But, so numerous were these previous issues that it is unlikely that any will have collector value in the forseeable future.

MINTING U.S. COINS

When the first US mint went into operation in 1793, coins were made entirely by hand, and, as there were many different steps from the die to the finished product, there were many possibilities for error. Despite the care taken, some mistakes did occur, to the great annoyance of the minters, and these early errors are highly prized by collectors.

By the mid-nineteenth century, mechanical processes had come into use, which virtually eliminated the manual procedures of older times. (Today, only the date and mintmark are still punched in by hand). Errors were few and some collectors specialized only in these.

Today, however, the picture has changed completely. Mintage figures for small denominations are now into the billions, and errors are far more common; so common, in fact, that few if any bring any significant premiums. But despite their lowered value, they are still highly prized. People seem to enjoy owning some tangible evidence of governments' imperfection!

LOCATION OF MINTS AND MINT MARKS

By act of Congress, the first United States mint was established in 1792, in Philadelphia, Pa. This was followed by six other acts of Congress, putting into operation six more mints throughout the U.S.

Mint marks, designating where the coin was made, are shown on the front or back (the obverse and the reverse), as follows:

"P" Philadelphia mint, operating from 1793 to date. However, coins minted here do not bear the mint mark, (prior to 1980), except for "wartime" nickels which were minted between 1942 and 1945. The mint mark "P" appears on the reverse of the five-cent piece, above the dome.

"C" Charlotte, N.C. The mint mark appears only on gold coins dated 1838 to 1861.

"CC" Carson City, Nevada. Coins from 1870 to 1893.

"D" Dahlonega, Ga. The "D" appears only on gold coins dated 1838 to 1861.

"D" Denver, Colo. Coins from 1906 to date.

"O" New Orleans, La. Coins from 1838 to 1861 and 1879 to 1909.

"S" San Francisco, Cal. Coins from 1854 to 1955, and 1968 to date.

ALLOY CONTENT IN U.S. COINS

From the time the first U.S. coins were minted, up to the year 1964, the one-cent pieces contained 95% copper and 5% tin/zinc. Five-cent pieces were made of 75% copper and 25% nickel. Silver coins contained 90% silver and 10% copper. However, there were some exceptions, as in 1943 when the one-cent piece was made of steel coated with zinc and the five-cent pieces of 1942 to 1945 were 35% silver, 56% copper and 9% manganese. These coins (the one-cent piece without copper and the five-cent piece without nickel) were known as "wartime coins"

CLAD OR SANDWICH COINS

Clad (also called sandwich) coins came into being in 1965, and are still being minted with the following alloy content: the outer coat of dimes, quarters, half dollars and dollars are 75% copper and 25% nickel; the inner core is 100% copper.

PROOF COINS

Proof coins are minted especially for collectors, who order the sets directly from the mint and pay a price higher than the face value of the coins. To achieve the bright surface and clearly defined details of a proof coin, slower hydraulic presses are used. The planchets are of perfect metal, and the dies are engraved and polished with extreme care. While other coins are struck only once, proof coins get two strikes to emphasize the smallest details of the design.

MINT ERRORS

In 1955, an error occurred (due to rotated hub doubling) on the one-cent piece which showed a double design on the coin. Buyers were stimulated by this coin as an interesting addition to their collections; they felt this was a once-in-a-lifetime find. However, the same error did happen again in 1972 when a double design occurred in the Lincoln one-cent piece. In the illustration shown here, you can see how the die shifted to produce a double image.

This is a true mint error, to be differentiated from a manufacturing error as described on page 6.

In the former, the error is in the die, and the error is faithfully reproduced on all coins struck by that die. The latter is the product of poor manufacture, that which in other products would be called a reject, or a "lemon", and is of little or no extra value

Not all coins with mint errors are equally regarded by collectors, and dealers, and not all sell at the high prices which one thinks they will command. So the coin with a mint error has to be considered not just for its error, but for other factors such as denomination, date and quantity available.

BUYING AND SELLING

It is virtually impossible today to put together a meaningful or valuable coin collection by going through your change. Due to the increased popularity of collecting, as well as all the publicity numismatics has received in recent years, practically nothing remains in circulation which is worth collecting. Therefore, the professional dealer has become the hub around which all numismatics revolve. Not only does he buy and sell coins for collectors, he is also a valuable source of information on coin shows and bourses, coin finds, new books, and more. Therefore beginning (as well as veteran) collectors are well-advised to strike a rapport with a dealer they trust.

New collectors should attempt to purchase the best coin of any type that they can afford. It is always better to buy one coin than ten for the same money, for the better conditioned pieces rise at a faster percentage than the worn specimens. Haste in purchasing is to be avoided, and bargains usually turn out to be far less than that. Due to publications such as this one, the value of any coin is easily ascertained. Anything too cheap usually has flaws that lessen its market value. When you go into the market to buy coins, be prepared with the approximate value of the coins you are seeking.

Coins may be bought or sold through Millers Mint Ltd., 313 E. Main St., Patchogue, N.Y. 11713 or Harmer Rooke Numismatists Ltd., 3 E. 57 St., New York, N.Y. 10022. Please do not send coins without writing first, including a stamped, self-addressed envelope, without which no inquiries will be answered. For further information see the last page.

HOW TO GRADE COINS

Nothing has more bearing on the value of a coin today than its condition. Truly uncirculated pieces can be worth hundreds of times more than worn specimens of the same date and mint. To put its importance in proper perspective, compare a coin to a used car. The more mileage, the less value is standard for automobiles, and the same holds true for coins. Therefore, it behooves the collector to spend the time to become proficient in grading. Knowledge is the best safeguard against overpaying. Following are the accepted grades in use today:

PROOF—Not a condition but a manner of striking. Coins struck as proofs exist in all grades. Prices listed are for uncirculated grade.

UNCIRCULATED—A coin which has never been used. It may show bagmarks, or slight scuffs from careless shipment but cannot show any wear on the highpoints.

ALMOST UNCIRCULATED (AU)—will show only the slightest rubs on the highest points. Must have some traces of original mint lustre.

EXTREMELY FINE (EF or XF)—All details are present and sharp, all letters bold, fields scarred or scuffed only very minimally.

VERY FINE (VF)—The lowest grades on which all details are visible. Some blurring or thickening of the smallest details is present. Minor defects in the fields and edges are acceptable.

FINE (F)—Well circulated, smallest details, tiniest letters are worn smooth. There may be considerable scuffing in the fields, slight edge nicks, etc.

VERY GOOD (VG)—All fine details, smaller letters are worn smooth. Fields and edges show considerable wear.

GOOD (G)—A well worn coin lacking all details. Profile and inner edges should be defined. Edges and fields could show slight damage, etc.

FAIR (F)—Just identifiable. If date does not show, coin is poor.

Please note that the above conditions reflect normal wear caused by the circulation for which the coin was originally minted. Coins which are holed, soldered, used in jewelry, bent, have graffiti or are mutilated in any way do not fit into any of the above categories and, depending on the extent of the damage, are worth only fractions of decent specimens. Conversely, pristine examples of uncirculated coins, particularly earlier dates, sell for considerably more than the prices quoted in this guide.

AN EXAMPLE OF GRADING

This is an example of how one goes about grading a coin. This Lincoln one-cent piece's high spots are the hair, ear and cheek, also the wheat stalks on the reverse. The first thing you do is to notice the high spots, where it is usual for wear to take place.

Now, using the symbols on the preceding page, you would arrive at your grading in this manner:

EF (Extra fine). The high spots on the obverse and reverse of the coin show some wear.

VF (Very fine). The jawbone and cheek are somewhat flattened. The ends and leaves of the wheat stalk on reverse do not show signs of wear.

F (Fine). Signs of wear appear on the wheat stalk.

VG (Very good). Wear is seen on the wheat stalk's leaves, and some part of the ends show heavy wear.

G (Good). The date, mottoes, rim and ends of the wheat stalk are worn.

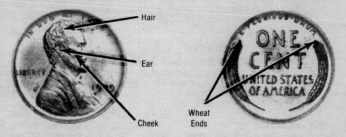

In the lists starting on page 14, you will notice a blank box preceding each item. In this little box mark the symbol of the grading you give to the coin, if you have it in your collection, and if you like to systematize your records.

CLEANING COINS

Probably more coins are ruined by improper cleaning than by any other factor. Imparting a shine to a coin does not restore missing details any more than shining a car will take out dents. Unless you are an expert, do not attempt to clean a coin. Dirt or tarnish will not decrease its value to any knowledgeable buyer.

Among substances which must NEVER be used to clean a coin are: Steel wool, sandpaper or emery cloth, toothpaste, scouring powder, or any preparation containing any abrasive at all, electrolytic vibration, pencil erasers, picks of any type or anything which could mar the (surprisingly) delicate surface of a coin. Proper cleaning of a coin (in those few instances where such is recommended) consists of LIFTING the dirt from a coin, not grinding.

GUIDE TO COINS AND PRICES

Mintage figures listed on the following pages are in thousands, making it necessary to add three zeros to arrive at the proper number. Where the mintage figure is of a lesser amount, this is noted.

The column headed A.D.P. indicates the price a dealer might give for the listed coin in the listed condition, very fine being about the lowest collectable grade (except for rarities.)

Please bear in mind that prices quoted in this book are intended as a guide only, based on averages gathered from the coin markets of the U.S. The price you may receive for (or be charged for) a specific coin can vary somewhat due to a number of conditions including saleability, popularity, local economic conditions, or how many a particular dealer might have in stock at a given time. Prices quoted herein comprise only "ball-park" figures.

HALF CENTS 1793-1857

The smallest denomination coin struck by the United States, these weigh 104 grams (1793-95) in new condition, are made of copper and measure 7/8″ in diameter.

LIBERTY CAP 1793-1797

DATE	Mintages in 1000's	A.D.P. (F)	Good	Fine	V.Fine	E.Fine
H1 ☐ 1793 Obv. Face Lft.	35	1,200	1,500	2,500	3,500	6,200
H2 ☐ 1794 Obv. Face Rt.	82	300	275	550	1,000	1,700
H3 ☐ 1795 Lettered Edge	26	200	210	475	900	1,500
H5 ☐ 1795 Plain Edge	109	200	200	450	850	1,400
H7 ☐ 1796 Pole to Cap	5	3,500	2,000	5,000	7,000	10,000
H8 ☐ 1796 No Pole	1,390	5,000		RARE		
H9 ☐ 1797 Lettered Edge		300	200	600	1,500	3,250
H10 ☐ 1797 Plain Edge	119	200	210	475	850	1,500

1794-1797

DRAPED BUST 1800-1808

H13 ☐ 1800	212	20	30	42	70	160
H15 ☐ 1802	14	150	150	300	900	4,000
H16 ☐ 1803	98	18	27	40	60	150

Coins on porous planchets are worth about half the listed values.

HALF CENTS - DRAPED BUST 1804-1808 (Con't.)

DATE	Mintages in 1000's	A.D.P. (F)	Good	Fine	V.Fine	E.Fine
H17 ☐ 1804 Spiked Chin		17	27	42	60	160
H18 ☐ 1804† Crosslet 4	1,055	15	25	40	55	150
H19 ☐ 1804* Plain 4		15	25	40	55	150
H21 ☐ 1805 Small 5 with stems . . .		17	27	42	60	160
H22 ☐ 1805 All other kinds	814	17	27	42	60	160
H24 ☐ 1806 Small 6 with stems . . .		60	40	100	200	650
H25 ☐ 1806 All other kinds	356	15	25	40	55	150
H27 ☐ 1807	476	17	27	40	75	175
H28 ☐ 1808 Over 7		75	50	125	300	1,250
H29 ☐ 1808	400	17	25	40	65	175

*With stemmed wreath reverse - double all prices

†Stemless wreath reverse commands slightly higher prices

HALF CENTS - CLASSIC HEAD 1809-1826

H30 ☐ 1809	1,155	17	27	42	55	125
H31 ☐ 1809/6		17	25	40	55	100
H33 ☐ 1810	215	17	30	45	65	150
H34 ☐ 1811	63	125	75	225	450	1,500
H35 ☐ 1811 Restrike Reverse of 1802		2,500	unc.	only	3,500	-
H36 ☐ 1825	63	16	25	35	60	85

Date	Mintages in 1000's	A.D.P. (F)	Good	Fine	V.Fine	Ex.Fine	Unc.	Proof
H37 ☐ 1826	234	12	20	28	40	55	325	
H38 ☐ 1828 13 Stars ..	12	20	28	40	60	275		
H39 ☐ 1828 12 Stars ..	606	14	22	35	60	175	500	
H40 ☐ 1829	487	13	20	25	40	60	275	
H41 ☐ 1831	(2,200)				1,000	1,600	3,000	5,000
☐ Lg. Berries....		1,700						3,750
☐ Sm. Berries ...		2,500						4,000
H42 ☐ 1832	154	12	20	28	40	55	275	
H43 ☐ 1833	120	12	22	35	40	60	275	
H44 ☐ 1834	141	12	20	28	40	55	275	
H45 ☐ 1835	398	12	20	28	40	55	275	
H46 ☐ 1836	(950) Proof Only					2,500		
☐ 1836 Restrike ..	(1,650) Proof Only					3,500		
☐ 1837 Token ...		15	20	30	50	75	300	

BRAIDED HAIR TYPE 1840-1857

☐ 1840		
☐ 1841 Proofs only		
☐ 1842 original		
☐ 1843 and		
☐ 1844 restrikes	2,400	4,00-6,000
☐ 1845 no records		
☐ 1846 of mintage		
☐ 1847 exist		
☐ 1848		
☐ 1849		

H68 ☐ 1849 Lg. Dt. . . .	40	14	27	35	52	70	300
H69 ☐ 1850	40	13	25	35	50	65	290
H70 ☐ 1851	147	13	25	35	50	65	285
H71 ☐ 1852		1,000					1,750
H72 ☐ 1853	130	13	25	35	50	65	285
H73 ☐ 1854	55	13	25	35	50	65	285
H74 ☐ 1855	56	13	25	35	50	65	285
H75 ☐ 1856	40	18	30	40	52	70	325
H76 ☐ 1857	35	22	32	45	60	85	350

Only Proof Coins ORIGINAL AND RESTRIKES Struck from 1840 to 1849   2,500

LARGE CENTS 1793-1857

Cents, often called "pennies", are probably the most popular of U.S. coins from a collecting standpoint. Not only does the wide range of dates cover the entire history of the U.S., but there are also enough varieties to satisfy that collector who delights in research. Additionally, in the earliest days, even the poorest numismatist could afford to collect cents, thus establishing a precedence which has not changed in 150 years. The size and weight of the cent has been altered five times since the first issues of 1793, scaling down to its present size in accordance with its popularity and importance to the country's economic picture.

Please note that large cents, particularly previous to 1816, often are found on porous planchets. Such coins are worth about half the listed values.

LARGE CENTS - FLOWING HAIR 1793

DATE	Mintages in 1000's	A.D.P. (F)	Good	V.Good	Fine	V.Fine	E.Fine
P1 ☐1793	36	2,100	2,000	2,700		3,500	6,500
Chain AMERI Reverse							
P2 ☐1793		1,600	1,400	2,000		2,750	4,800
Chain AMERICA Reverse							
P3 ☐1793		1,500	1,350	2,000		2,750	4,800
Chain reverse. Periods after date of Liberty obverse							
P6 ☐1793	63	1,000	900	1,200		1,700	2,750
Wreath reverse, edge has vines and bars							
P7 ☐1793		800	750	1,250		1,800	2,500
Wreath reverse, lettered edge double leaf on edge							
P8 ☐1793		1,000	950	1,250		1,800	2,800
Wreath reverse, lettered edge one leaf on edge							

LIBERTY CAP 1793-1796

1793 Liberty Cap Type

LARGE CENT - LIBERTY CAP 1793-1796

DATE	Mintages in 1000's	A.D.P. (F)	Good	V.Good	Fine	V.Fine	E.Fine
P9 ☐1793 Liberty Cap	11	1,200	1,000	1,500	2,500	5,000	17,000
P10 ☐1794 "Head of 1793"* ..	919	110	250	400	900	2,400	5,000
P11 ☐1794 "Head of 1794"• ..		150	125	175	300	600	1,000
P12 ☐1794 "Head of 1795" ...		150	125	175	300	600	1,000
P13 ☐1794 Starred Rev.		3,000	1,800	2,800	6,000	12,000	22,000

One Cent
In Center
Of Wreath

One Cent
High in
Wreath

P18 ☐1795 LTD Edge*	37	150	125	200	300	600	1,700
P23 ☐1795 Plain Edge*	501	75	75	100	200	350	600
P26 ☐1796 Liberty Cap	110	50	75	100	200	300	600

*ONE CENT — in Center of Wreath   •ONE CENT — High in Wreath

LIHERTY
ERROR 1796

DATE	Mintages in 1000's	A.D.P. (F)	Good	V.Good	Fine	V.Fine	E.Fine
P28 ☐1796	363	100	60	75	125	250	600
P29 ☐1796 LIHERTY		200	100	125	300	500	1,500
P36 ☐1797 Stemmed Wreath . .		60	35	50	110	225	600
P37 ☐1797 Stemless	898	110	45	85	140	250	700
P40 ☐1798/7 Over 97		90	40	100	175	400	900
P44 ☐1798 Large Dt.	1,842	40	35	50	90	250	650
P49 ☐1799 Normal Dt.	42	950	350	600	1,750	3,500	6,500
P50 ☐1800 Over 1798†		50	25	40	80	225	650
P51 ☐1800 Over 179	2,822	45	22	35	75	220	600
P52 ☐1800 normal date		45	22	35	75	220	600
P54 ☐1801 Blunt "1"		45	22	35	75	220	600
P57 ☐1801 Perfect "1"	1,363	45	22	35	75	220	600
P59 ☐1801 3 errors (1/1000 . . one stem. united)		125	50	75	200	500	1,000

LARGE CENT - DRAPED BUST 1801-1804

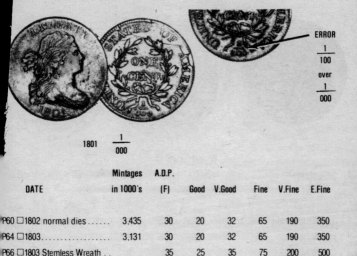

ERROR

$$\frac{1}{100}$$ over $$\frac{1}{000}$$

1801 $$\frac{1}{000}$$

DATE	Mintages in 1000's	A.D.P. (F)	Good	V.Good	Fine	V.Fine	E.Fine
P60 ☐1802 normal dies	3,435	30	20	32	65	190	350
P64 ☐1803	3,131	30	20	32	65	190	350
P66 ☐1803 Stemless Wreath . .		35	25	35	75	200	500
P70 ☐1804 Normal Dies	96	500	350	500	900	1,800	3,600

LARGE CENTS - DRAPED BUST - 1804-1807

1804
Normal Die

1804
Restrike
of 1860

DATE	Mintages in 1000's	A.D.P. (F)	Good	V.Good	Fine	V.Fine	E.Fine
P71 ☐ 1804 Restrike of 1860 ..		200	Unc. only		400		
P72 ☐ 1805 Blunt "1" in Date ..	941	35	22	35	75	200	400
P74 ☐ 1806	348	45	38	60	80	250	750
P75 ☐ 1807 Over 6 lg. 7		35	20	32	65	140	400

Small Fraction   Large Fraction   COMET VARIETY, 1807

	Mintages in 1000's	A.D.P. (F)	Good	V.Good	Fine	V.Fine	E.Fine
P77 ☐ 1807 Lg.Fr.	829	35	20	30	60	125	375
P79 ☐ 1807 Sm.Fr.		40	25	40	70	175	500
P80 ☐ 1807 Comet		45	30	45	80	195	650

DATE	Mintages in 1000's	A.D.P. (F)	Good	V.Good	Fine	V.Fine	E.Fine
P81 ☐ 1808	1.007	40	27	40	75	250	600
P82 ☐ 1809	223	125	60	90	200	500	950
P83 ☐ 1810 Over 9	1.459	35	25	35	70	225	550
P84 ☐ 1810		25	23	32	65	220	535
P85 ☐ 1811 Over 10	218	80	50	85	175	400	900
P86 ☐ 1811		90	45	80	165	375	850
P88 ☐ 1812	1.076	25	25	35	70	225	550
P89 ☐ 1813	418	55	35	60	100	275	650
P91 ☐ 18 4 Plain 4	358	30	25	35	70	225	550
P92 ☐ 18 4 Crosslet 4		30	25	35	70	225	550

DATE	Mintages in 1000's	A.D.P. (VF)	Fine	V.Fine	Ex.Fine	Au.	Unc.
P93 ☐1816	2,821	15	14	30	70	150	350
P94 ☐1817	3,948	10	12	20	65	140	300
P97 ☐1817 15 Stars		20	25	45	75	175	450
P98 ☐1818	3,167	10	12	20	65	135	300
P100 ☐1819 Over 18		10	12	20	65	150	325
P101 ☐1819	2,671	10	12	20	65	140	300
P103 ☐1820 Over 19		10	12	20	65	170	375
P104 ☐1820	4,408	8	10	20	65	150	350
P107 ☐1821		75	50	150	400	900	2,500
P109 ☐1822	2,072	10	12	20	65	140	300
P110 ☐1823 Over 22		90	60	150	350	800	RARE
P111 ☐1823 Normal dt.	856	150	125	200	600	1,750	RARE
P113 ☐1824 Over 22		30	30	75	200	700	4,000
P114 ☐1824	1,193	18	15	35	80	500	2,000
P117 ☐1825	1,461	15	15	30	75	175	450

Cents dated 1816-1857 in red unc. command higher prices, but are not usually collectable in grades below fine.

1823 Normal

1823
Restrike
Broken Die

DATE	Mintages in 1000's	A.D.P. (VF)	Fine	V.Fine	Ex.Fine	Au.	Unc.
P118 ☐ 1826 Over 25.........		35	30	60	150	250	700
P119 ☐ 1826.................	1.517	12	12	22	65	140	300
P121 ☐ 1827.................	2.358	11	11	20	65	135	275
P122 ☐ 1828 Large Date......	2.261	11	11	20	65	150	300
P124 ☐ 1828 Small Date......		25	25	45	90	200	500
P125 ☐ 1829.................	1.415	12	14	25	70	175	325
P127 ☐ 1830 Large Ltrs.......	1.712	12	14	25	70	175	325
P128 ☐ 1830 Small Ltrs.......		40	45	75	160	450	1,000
P129 ☐ 1831.................	3.359	10	11	20	65	135	275

DATE	Mintages in 1000's	A.D.P. (VF)	Fine	V.Fine	Ex.Fine	Av.	Unc.
P131 ☐ 1832	2.362	10	12	20	65	150	275
P132 ☐ 1833	2.739	10	12	20	65	150	250
P133 ☐ 1834	1.855	10	12	20	65	150	275
P137 ☐ 1835	3.878	10	12	20	65	150	275
P139 ☐ 1835 Type of 1836		13	15	25	80	175	350
P140 ☐ 1836	2.111	10	12	20	65	150	250
P142 ☐ 1837	5.558	10	12	20	65	150	250
P144 ☐ 1838	6.370	10	12	20	65	150	250

Booby Head

DATE	Mintages in 1000's	A.D.P. (VF)	Fine	V.Fine	Ex.Fine	Av.	Unc.
P145 ☐ 1839 Over 36		200	200	400	1,000	RARE	—
P147 ☐ 1839 Silly Head	3,120	9	15	30	75	175	500
P148 ☐ 1839 Booby Head		8	12	20	65	150	325
P151 ☐ 1840	2,463	7	11	20	65	120	225
P154 ☐ 1841	1,597	7	9	16	45	115	275
P155 ☐ 1842	2,383	7	9	15	40	115	225

LARGE CENTS - BRAIDED HAIR, 1843-1857

DATE	Mintages in 1000's	A.D.P. (VF)	V.Fine	Ex.Fine	Av.	Unc.
P151 ☐ 1843		6	15	40	100	250
P158 ☐ 1843 Obv. 1842 .... All Kinds						
Or Rev. 1844	2,428	23	55	90	175	450
P160 ☐ 1844....................		6	12	40	100	225
P161 ☐ 1844 Over 81	2,399	6	35	45	150	500
P162 ☐ 1845....................	3,895	6	14	40	100	250
P165 ☐ 1846....................	4,121	6	14	40	100	250
P167 ☐ 1847	6,183	6	14	40	100	250
P170 ☐ 1848....................	6,415	6	14	40	100	250
P173 ☐ 1849....................	4,178	6	14	50	125	275
P174 ☐ 1850....................	4,426	6	14	50	125	300
P175 ☐ 1851....................	9,899	6	14	50	125	250
P176 ☐ 1851 Over 81		10	20	50	175	450
P177 ☐ 1852	5,063	6	14	40	100	200
P179 ☐ 1853....................	6,641	6	14	40	100	200
P180 ☐ 1854....................	4,236	6	14	40	100	210
P181 ☐ 1855*...................	1,575	6	14	40	100	225
P185 ☐ 1856*		6	15	40	100	275
P187 ☐ 1857**	333	20	40	65	125	400

Usually collected in very fine or better.
*upright or slanting "5"s
**large & small dates

SMALL CENTS - FLYING EAGLE, 1856- TO DATE

By the 1850's, both the half cent and large cent had fallen into disfavor with the public due to their scant purchasing power, and the bulges they made in pockets because of the amounts that had to be carried around. Consequently, Congress enacted legislation to mint the smaller size coin, these proving so popular that, although the thickness was changed in 1864, the diameter has remained the same since.

FLYING EAGLE, 1856-1858

Large Letters

Small Letters

DATE	Mintages in 1000's	A.D.P. (VF)	V.Good	Fine	V.Fine	Ex.Fine	Av.	Unc.
P189 ☐1856 Approx. .	1	850	800	1,000	1,200	1,500	1,800	3,500
P190 ☐1857	17,450	10	10	13	25	55	140	250
P193 ☐1858 Sm.Ltrs.	24,600	10	10	13	25	55	140	240
P192 ☐1858 Lg. Ltrs.		10	10	13	25	55	140	240

*Proofs struck in 1856 — 1858 $4,000

Designed by James B. Longacre, the popular "Indian Pennies" were first issued in 1859 and continued to be minted until superceded by the Lincoln Cents in 1909. From the first issue through 1864, these cents were composed of copper and nickel. In 1864, they were reduced in weight and thickness and the composition was changed to bronze which remained until 1982, when they were changed to copper-plated zinc.

DATE	Mintages in 1000's	A.D.P. (VF)	V. Good	Fine	V. Fine	Ex. Fine	AU	Unc.	Proof
P195 ☐ 1859	36,400	10	5	8	17	50	125	300	1,100
P198 ☐ 1860	20,566	4	4	6	10	20	35	150	800
P199 ☐ 1861	10,100	11	10	13	20	35	55	200	750
P200 ☐ 1862	28,075	4	3	5	9	18	35	100	750
P201 ☐ 1863	49,840	4	3	5	8	16	30	100	750
P202 ☐ 1864									
Copper-Nickel ...	13,740	7	7	11	15	26	50	150	800
P203 ☐ 1864 Bronze	39,234	6	4	7	12	20	30	75	1,000
P205 ☐ 1864 L on Ribbon		40	25	40	65	90	150		275—
P207 ☐ 1865	35,429	5	4	6	10	17	25	45	500
P209 ☐ 1866	9,827	25	18	25	40	60	90	135	400
P210 ☐ 1867	9,821	25	18	25	40	60	90	135	400
P212 ☐ 1868	10,267	25	18	25	40	60	89	135	400
P213 ☐ 1869 Over 8		175	·75	160	250	375	500	900	—
P214 ☐ 1869	6,420	50	26	55	80	110	165	275	600
P215 ☐ 1870	5,275	35	25	40	60	85	115	185	425
P216 ☐ 1871	3,929	40	30	50	70	95	135	200	475
P217 ☐ 1872	4,042	55	35	65	95	125	175	275	550
P218 ☐ 1873	11,676	13	7	15	25	45	60	100	350.
P221 ☐ 1874	14,187	13	7	15	25	45	60	100	300
P222 ☐ 1875	13,528	13	7	15	25	45	60	100	300
P223 ☐ 1876	7,944	16	12	20	30	50	70	110	300
P224 ☐ 1877	852	250	200	250	350	500	750	1,300	2,500

SMALL CENTS - INDIAN HEAD, 1878-1909 (Cont'd.)

DATE	Mintages in 1000's	A.D.P. (VF)	Fine	V.Fine	Ex.Fine	AU	Unc.	Proof
P225 ☐ 1878	5,800	20	25	40	60	75	110	200
P226 ☐ 1879	16,231	4	6	10	19	28	50	200
P227 ☐ 1880	38,965	1	3	4	10	17	38	200
P228 ☐ 1881	39,211	1	3	4	10	17	38	200
P229 ☐ 1882	38,581	1	3	4	10	17	38	200
P230 ☐ 1883	45,598	1	3	4	10	17	38	200
P231 ☐ 1884	23,262	2	4	7	14	20	45	200
P232 ☐ 1885	11,765	5	7	12	21	30	60	250
P233 ☐ 1886	17,654	3	5	7	14	24	50	200
P234 ☐ 1887	45,226	.75	1.75	3	9	15	35	200
P235 ☐ 1888	37,494	.75	1.75	3	9	15	35	200
P236 ☐ 1889	48,860	.75	1.75	3	9	15	35	200
P237 ☐ 1890	57,183	.75	1.75	3	9	15	35	150
P238 ☐ 1891	47,072	.75	1.75	3	9	15	35	150
P239 ☐ 1892	37,650	.75	1.75	3	9	15	35	150
P240 ☐ 1893	46,642	.75	1.75	3	9	15	35	150
P241 ☐ 1894	16,752	2	4	6	12	16	40	150
P243 ☐ 1895	38,344	.75	1.50	2	8	12	35	150
P244 ☐ 1896	39,057	.75	1.50	2	8	12	35	150
P245 ☐ 1897	50,466	.75	1.50	2	8	12	35	150
P246 ☐ 1898	49,823	.75	1.50	2	8	12	35	150
P247 ☐ 1899	53,600	.75	1.50	2	8	12	35	150
P248 ☐ 1900	66,834	.75	1	2	8	12	35	150
P249 ☐ 1901	76,611	.75	1	2	6	12	35	150
P250 ☐ 1902	87,377	.75	1	2	6	12	35	150
P251 ☐ 1903	85,094	.75	1	2	6	12	35	150
P252 ☐ 1904	61,328	.75	1	2	6	12	35	150
P253 ☐ 1905	80,719	.75	1	2	6	12	35	150
P254 ☐ 1906	96,022	.75	1	2	6	12	35	150
P255 ☐ 1907	108,139	.75	1	2	6	12	35	150
P256 ☐ 1908	32,328	.75	1	2	6	12	35	150
P257 ☐ 1908S	1,115	10	25	30	40	75	125	—
P258 ☐ 1909	14,371	.75	1	2	8	12	35	250
P259 ☐ 1909S	309	60	125	150	200	250	350	—

SMALL CENTS - LINCOLN HEAD 1909-1915

Issued to commemorate the 100th anniversary of the birth of Abraham Lincoln. The inclusion of the designer's initials ("VDB" for Victor D. Brenner) caused some indignation on the part of the general public resulting in their removal and thereby creating some interesting early varieties.

1909 TO DATE

No V.D.B.

V.D.B. 1918 on   Mint Mark

DATE	Mintages in 1000's	A.D.P. (VF)	V.Fine	Ex.Fine	AU	Unc.	Matte Proof
P260 ☐ 1909 V.D.B.	27,997	.75	3	4	6	11	500
P261 ☐ 1909S V.D.B.	484	150	300	335	400	475	
P262 ☐ 1909	72,703		1.50	2	5	14	300
P263 ☐ 1909S	1,825	30	60	80	120	175	
P264 ☐ 1910	146,801	—	.50	1.50	4	12	300
P265 ☐ 1910S	6,045	5	10	18	40	90	
P266 ☐ 1911	101,178	—	1	2	6	15	300
P267 ☐ 1911D	12,672	4	9	19	40	90	
P268 ☐ 1911S	4,026	8	17	28	55	100	
P269 ☐ 1912	68,153	1	3.50	5	8	20	300
P270 ☐ 1912D	10,411	4	11	25	45	100	
P271 ☐ 1912S	4,431	7	15	24	44	100	
P272 ☐ 1913	76,532	—	1.75	4	7	20	300
P273 ☐ 1913D	15,804	2	5	15	32	70	
P274 ☐ 1913S	6,101	5	10	17	45	80	
P275 ☐ 1914	74,238	1	2.75	5	14	50	300
P276 ☐ 1914D	1,193	70	140	300	525	900	
P277 ☐ 1914S	4,137	7	15	25	55	150	
P278 ☐ 1915	29,092	1.50	4	22	45	90	350

Except for rare dates and mintmarks, generally collected in very fine condition or better.

DATE	Mintages in 1000's	A.D.P. (EF)	V.Fine	Ex.Fine	AU	Unc.
P279 ☐ 1915D	22,050	2	2.50	7	15	35
P280 ☐ 1915S	4,834	5	10	19	38	85
P281 ☐ 1916 (PF 250)	131,839	1		2	3	9
P282 ☐ 1916D	35,956	2		5	10	50
P283 ☐ 1916S	22,510	2		6	14	55
P284 ☐ 1917	196,430	1		2	4	11
P285 ☐ 1917D	55,120	2	2	4	12	45
P286 ☐ 1917S	32,620	2	2	5	15	50
P287 ☐ 1918	288,105	1		2	5	12
P288 ☐ 1918D	47,830	2	2	4	12	45
P289 ☐ 1918S	34,680	2	2	5	14	50
P290 ☐ 1919	392,021	.50		1.50	4	8
P291 ☐ 1919D	57,154	2	2	3	8	40
P292 ☐ 1919S	139,760	1		2	6	28
P293 ☐ 1920	310,165	1		2	4	8
P294 ☐ 1920D	49,280	2		3	9	50
P295 ☐ 1920S	46,220	2		3	10	50
P296 ☐ 1921	39,157	2		3	8	35
P297 ☐ 1921S	15,274	5	2.50	10	50	110
P298 ☐ 1922 (No Mint Mark)		200	450	750	1,500	4,000
P299 ☐ 1922D	7,160	5	8	16	35	80
P300 ☐ 1923	74,723	1	1.50	2	3	9
P301 ☐ 1923S	8,700	5	4	11	55	160
P302 ☐ 1924	75,178	1		2	5	22
P303 ☐ 1924D	2,520	16	12	35	90	210
P304 ☐ 1924S	11,696	3	2	4	20	100
P305 ☐ 1925	139,949	1		1.50	3	8
P306 ☐ 1925D	22,580	2		3	9	40
P307 ☐ 1925S	26,380	1		2	12	52
P308 ☐ 1926	157,088	1		1.50	2.50	6

DATE	Mintages in 1000's	A.D.P. (Unc.)	Ex.Fine	AU	Unc.	Proof
P309 ☐ 1926D	28,022	20	3	10	40	
P310 ☐ 1926S	4,550	60	9	40	100	
P311 ☐ 1927	144,440	3	1.75	3	7	
P312 ☐ 1927D	27,170	15	2.50	7	24	
P313 ☐ 1927S	14,276	30	3	15	55	
P314 ☐ 1928	134,116	3	1.50	3	7	
P315 ☐ 1928D	31,170	10	2	6	18	
P316 ☐ 1928S	17,266	25	3	10	42	
P317 ☐ 1929	185,262	3	.75	1.75	4	
P318 ☐ 1929D	41,730	7	1.50	3	14	
P319 ☐ 1929S	50,148	4	1	2.50	8	
P320 ☐ 1930	157,415	2	.75	1.75	4	
P321 ☐ 1930D	40,100	4	1.50	4	10	
P322 ☐ 1930S	24,286	3	1	2	6	
P323 ☐ 1931	19,396	8	1.50	5	15	
P324 ☐ 1931D	4,480	30	7	23	45	
P325 ☐ 1931S	886	45	40	50	75	
P326 ☐ 1932	9,062	8	2.75	5	15	
P327 ☐ 1932D	10,500	7	2	3.50	14	
P328 ☐ 1933	14,360	7	2	4	14	
P329 ☐ 1933D	6,200	9	3	6	18	
P330 ☐ 1934	219,080	-	25	1.50	7	
P331 ☐ 1934D	28,446	10	1	7	42	
P332 ☐ 1935	245,388				2.50	
P333 ☐ 1935D	47,000				7	
P334 ☐ 1935S	38,702	10			24	
P335 ☐ 1936	309,638				1	350
P336 ☐ 1936D	40,620	2			4	
P337 ☐ 1936S	29,130	2			4	
P338 ☐ 1937	309,179	1			2.50	250
P339 ☐ 1937D	50,430	2			3.50	
P340 ☐ 1937S	35,500	2			3.50	
P341 ☐ 1938	156,697	1			2	75
P342 ☐ 1938D	20,010	1			3	
P343 ☐ 1938S	15,180	2			4	
P344 ☐ 1939	316,480				1	50

DATE	Mintages in 1000's	A.D.P.	AU	Unc.	Proof
P345 ☐1939D	15,160		1	5.50	
P346 ☐1939S	52,070		1	2.50	
P347 ☐1940	586,826			1	30
P384 ☐1940D	81,390			2	
P349 ☐1940S	112,940			3	
P350 ☐1941	887,039			1	30
P351 ☐1941D	128,700		1	4	
P352 ☐1941S	92,360		1	4.50	
P353 ☐1942	667,829			.75	30
P354 ☐1942D	206,698			.80	
P355 ☐1942S	85,590		1	6	
WARTIME STEEL COMPOSITION					
P357 ☐1943	684,629			1	
P358 ☐1943D	217,660			2.25	
P359 ☐1943S	191,550			4.50	
BRONZE—REGULAR PRE-WAR COMPOSITION					
P360 ☐1944	1,435,400			.25	
P361 ☐1944D	430,578			.75	
P362 ☐1944S				.50	
P363 ☐1945	1,040,515			.25	
P364 ☐1945D	226,268			.75	
P365 ☐1945S	181,770			.60	
P366 ☐1946	991,665			.25	
P367 ☐1946D	315,690			.25	
P368 ☐1946S	198,100			.50	
P369 ☐1947	190,555			.75	
P370 ☐1947D	194,750			.25	
P371 ☐1947S	99,000			.75	
P372 ☐1948	317,570			.50	

Generally collected only in uncirculated condition.

DATE	Mintages in 1000's	A.D.P. (VF)	E.Fine	Unc.	Proof
P373 ☐1948D	172.637			.75	
P374 ☐1948S	81.735			1	
P375 ☐1949	217.490			1.25	
P376 ☐1949D	154.370			1	
P377 ☐1949S	64.290			2	
P378 ☐1950	272.686			1.25	50
P379 ☐1950D	334.950			.35	
P380 ☐1950S	118.505			.75	
P381 ☐1951	294.633			2.25	20
P382 ☐1951D	625.355			.40	
P383 ☐1951S	100.890			1.50	
P384 ☐1952	186.857			.50	15
P385 ☐1952D	746.130			.65	
P386 ☐1952S	137.800			.75	
P387 ☐1953	256.884			.25	15
P388 ☐1953D	700.515			.50	
P389 ☐1953S	181.835			.50	
P390 ☐1954	71.873			.50	6
P391 ☐1954D	251.552			.25	
P392 ☐1954S	96.190			.25	
P393 ☐1955	330.958			.25	3
P394 ☐1955 Double Die		175	400	600	
P395 ☐1955D	563.257			.25	
P396 ☐1955S	44.610			.50	
P397 ☐1956	421.414			.25	2
P398 ☐1956D	1.098.201			.25	
P399 ☐1957	283.788			.25	2
P400 ☐1957D	1.051.342			.25	
P401 ☐1958	253.401			.25	3
P402 ☐1958D	800.953			.25	

SMALL CENTS -LINCOLN MEMORIAL 1959 TO DATE

In 1959 the 150th anniversary of Lincoln's birth was observed by changing the design of the original Lincoln cent, and putting on the reverse the Lincoln Memorial in Washington, D.C.

1955/55
Double Die Obverse

The Mint Mark is on the Obverse under the date

1960 Small Date

DATE	Mintages in 1000's	Unc.	Proof	DATE	Mintages in 1000's	Unc.	Proof
P403 ☐ 1959	610,864	.20	1	P432 ☐ 1971	1,919,490	25	
P404 ☐ 1959D	1,279,760	.15		P433 ☐ 1971D	2,911,045	.20	
1960				P434 ☐ 1971S	528,354	.15	1
P405 ☐ Sm.Dt.	588,096	3	16	P435 ☐ 1972	2,933,250	.20	
P406 ☐ Lg.Dt.		25	1	P436 ☐ 1972 Double Die		225	
1960D				P437 ☐ 1972D	2,665,071	.20	1
P408 ☐ Sm.Dt.	1,580,885	.15		P438 ☐ 1972S	380,280	.15	1
P409 ☐ Lg.Dt.		2	20	P439 ☐ 1973	3,728,245	.15	
P410 ☐ 1961	756,373	.15	1	P440 ☐ 1973D	3,549,576	.15	
P411 ☐ 1961D	1,753,267	.15		P441 ☐ 1973S	319,937	.15	2
P413 ☐ 1962	609,263	.15	1	P442 ☐ 1974	4,232,140	.05	
P414 ☐ 1962D	1,793,148	.15		P443 ☐ 1974D	4,235,098	.05	
P415 ☐ 1963	757,148	.15	1	P444 ☐ 1974S	412,039	.20	2
P416 ☐ 1963D	1,744,020	.15		P445 ☐ 1975	545,147	.05	
P417 ☐ 1964	2,652,526	.15	1	P446 ☐ 1975D	45,052	.05	
P418 ☐ 1964D	3,799,071	.15		P447 ☐ 1975S(PF.only)	2,845,450*		12
P419 ☐ 1965	1,497,225	.15		P448 ☐ 1976	4,674,292,426*		
P420 ☐ 1966	2,188,148	.15		P449 ☐ 1976D	4,221,592,455*	.10	
P421 ☐ 1967	3,048,667	.15		P450 ☐ 1976S (PF.only)	4,149,730*		4

P422 ☐ 1968	1.707.881	.15		P451 ☐ 1977 ...... 4.469.930.000*		
P423 ☐ 1968D	2.886.270	.15		P452 ☐ 1977D 4.194.062.300*		
P424 ☐ 1968S	261.311	.20	1	P453 ☐ 1977S (PF only) 3.251.152*		4
P425 ☐ 1969	1.137.000	.35		P454 ☐ 1978 ...... 5.558.605.000*	.10	
P426 ☐ 1969D	4.003.000		4	P455 ☐ 1978D 4.280.233.400*	.10	
P427 ☐ 1969S	547.310	.20	1	P456 ☐ 1978S (PF only) 3.127.781*		5
P428 ☐ 1970	1.898.315	.15		P457 ☐ 1979		
P429 ☐ 1970D	2.891.439	.15		P458 ☐ 1979D		
P430 ☐ 1970S Sm.Dt...		.10	30	P459 ☐ 1979S		
P431 ☐ 1969S Lg. Dt...		.15	1	P460 ☐ 1980S (PF only)		2
				P461 ☐ 1981S (PF only)		6
				P462 ☐ 1982S (PF only)		4

TWO CENT PIECE - 1864-1873

The shortage of copper which occurred during the Civil War caused the general hoarding of cents and brought about the minting of the two-cent piece, which proved unpopular. This was our first coin with the motto "In God We Trust". The small motto of 1864 bears a stem on the leaf below "Trust", differentiating it from the more common large motto.

(First Coin to Bear the Motto "In God We Trust")

1864 Small Motto   1864 Large Motto

Date	Mintages in 1000's	A.D.P. (F)	Fine	V.Fine	Ex.Fine	AU	Unc.*	Proof
CT1 ☐Small Motto	19,848	50	85	135	225	350	600	
CT2 ☐Large Motto		3.50	7	12.50	30	60	200	550
CT5 ☐1865	13,640	3.50	7	12.50	30	60	200	400
CT9 ☐1866	3,177	4	7.50	14	30	62	225	400
CT11☐1867	2,939	3.50	7.50	14	30	65	235	400
CT12☐1868	2,804	3	7	15	34	70	250	400
CT14☐1869	1,547	4	9	16	35	75	300	400
CT15☐1870	861	9	16	30	60	90	350	450
CT16☐1871	721	10	20	35	75	115	350	475
CT17☐1872	65	75	140	200	300	400	800	525
CT18☐1873 Closed 3	(600)	500						1,400
CT19☐1873 Open 3								
(Restrike) ...	(480)	600 PROOFS	ONLY					1,600

*Red uncirculated coins (original color) command about 50% premiums.

THREE CENT PIECE - SILVER 1851-1873

Originally called a trime, this piece was created as a result of a change in the postal rates. They were popular until the Civil War when general hoarding drove them out of circulation. Those minted after 1862 were not intended for circulation.

DATE	Mintages in 1000's	A.D.P. (F)	Fine	V.Fine	Ex.Fine	AU	Unc.	Proof
ST1 ☐1851 Var.1 ..	5,447	8	15	25	45	110	300	
ST2 ☐1851 0	720	12	30	50	90	175	400	
ST3 ☐1852	18,663	8	15	25	45	110	300	
ST5 ☐1853	11,400	8	15	25	45	110	300	
ST6 ☐1854 Var.2 ..	671	12	20	35	85	200	350	
ST7 ☐1855	139	15	35	65	135	235	450	2,000
ST9 ☐1856	1,458	10	18	30	80	185	435	2,000
ST10 ☐1857	1,042	10	15	32	80	190	450	1,500
ST11 ☐1858	1,604	10	15	30	80	185	435	1,000
ST12 ☐1859 Var.3...	365	8	16	30	55	110	300	500
ST13 ☐1860	287	8	16	30	55	110	300	500
ST15 ☐1861	498	8	16	30	55	110	300	500
ST17 ☐1862	364	8	16	30	55	110	300	500
ST20 ☐1863	21						550	700
ST21 ☐1864	12						550	700
ST22 ☐1865	8						600	500
ST23 ☐1866	23						550	500
ST24 ☐1867	5		Circulated coins were				625	500
ST25 ☐1868	4		melted down with silver				625	500
ST26 ☐1869	5		bullion sold abroad.				625	500
ST27 ☐1870	4						625	500
ST28 ☐1871	4						625	500
ST29 ☐1872	2						700	500
ST30 ☐1873		Proofs only (600)						1,200

THREE CENT NICKEL, 1865-1889

DATE	Mintages in 1000's	A.D.P. (F)	Fine	V.Fine	Ex.Fine	AU	Unc.	Proof
NT1 ☐1865	11,382	3	6	8	14	30	115	500
NT3 ☐1866	4,801	3	6	8	14	30	115	250
NT4 ☐1867	3,915	3	6	8	14	30	115	250
NT6 ☐1868	3,252	3	6	8	15	30	125	250
NT8 ☐1869	1,604	3	6.50	8	15	32	125	250
NT10☐1870	1,335	3	6.75	8	16	34	125	250
NT12☐1871	604	3	8	10	17	38	135	275
NT13☐1872	862	3	7	9	16	35	125	275
NT14☐1873	1,173	3	6.50	8	16	34	125	275
NT16☐1874	790	3	7	9	16	38	135	275
NT17☐1875	228	5	10	14	25	65	175	300
NT18☐1876	162	7	14	20	32	75	200	300
NT19☐1877	(510)	750 Proof only						1250
NT20☐1878	2	250 Proof only						800
NT21☐1879	41	30	60	75	25	125	250	350
NT22☐1880	25	35	80	100	120	150	275	400
NT23☐1881	1,081	3	6	8	15	35	110	275
NT24☐1882	25	40	75	90	110	140	250	300
NT25☐1883	11	100	170	200	225	275	350	400
NT26☐1884	6	200	325	350	400	450	600	500
NT27☐1885	5	225	400	425	500	575	700	600
NT28☐1886	4	250 Proof only						600
NT30☐1887	8	200	325	350	385	440	550	550
NT29☐1887 over 86		Proof only						750
NT31☐1888	41	30	60	70	80	100	300	350
NT32☐1889	21	40	80	90	110	135	275	350

NICKELS -SHIELD, 1866-1883

1866-83

1866-67
with rays

1867-83
without rays

	DATE	Mintages in 1000's	A.D.P. (VF)	Fine	V.Fine	Ex.Fine	AU	Unc.	Proof
N1	☐1866	14,742	15	18	30	80	150	375	1400
N5	☐1867 w. rays	30,909	30	22	40	90	175	400	4,000
N6	☐1867 no rays		7	9	12	25	45	150	300
N9	☐1868	28,817	7	9	12	25	45	150	300
N12	☐1869	16,395	7	9	13	27	48	160	350
N13	☐1870	4,806	8	10	18	32	60	175	350
N14	☐1871	561	30	40	55	90	150	300	450
N15	☐1872	6,036	9	10	18	32	65	185	350
N19	☐1873	4,550	9	11	18	33	67	200	350
N21	☐1874	3,538	11	12	20	35	70	210	350
N22	☐1875	2,097	16	16	25	45	80	225	350
N23	☐1876	2,530	15	15	23	40	70	215	350
N24	☐1877	(500*)	700			PROOF ONLY			1200
N25	☐1878	2	300			PROOF ONLY			750
N26	☐1879	29	200	350	375	450	500	600	500
N28	☐1880	20	210	360	400	500	600	700	500
N29	☐1881	72	150	275	310	360	420	550	500
N30	☐1882	11,477	7	9	13	27	44	150	350
N33	☐1883	1,457	7	10	14	29	45	165	350
N31	☐1883 over 2		50	55	80	120	200	400	

*Total mintage.

In 1883 Charles E. Barber designed this five-cent piece considered one of the most beautiful U.S. coins.

Without "CENTS"

Mint Mark 1912
under Dot

The Roman numeral "V" is on the reverse, but the word CENTS did not appear on the first issue of the coin. Illegally, these nickels were sometimes gold plated and circulated as $5 gold pieces. Correction was made by adding CENTS below the wreath, E PLURIBUS UNUM above it.

	DATE	Mintages in 1000's	A.D.P. (VF)	Fine	V.Fine	Ex.Fine	AU	Unc.	Proof
N34	☐1883 no cents	5,480	2	3	5	7	12	50	400
N35	☐1883 with cents	16,033	8	10	16	30	60	150	350
N36	☐1884	11,274	10	10	18	32	60	160	350
N37	☐1885	1,476	260	400	550	700	800	1,000	1,200
N38	☐1886	3,330	60	100	150	200	300	450	700
N39	☐1887	15,264	5	10	14	27	55	150	250
N40	☐1888	10,720	10	12	20	33	70	160	250
N41	☐1889	15,881	6	8	14	28	55	150	250
N42	☐1890	16,259	6	9	15	28	58	160	250
N43	☐1891	16,834	7	8	14	27	55	150	250
N44	☐1892	11,700	8	8.50	16	30	58	160	250
N45	☐1893	13,370	7	8.50	15	27	55	150	250

DATE	Mintages in 1000's	A.D.P. (VF)	Fine	V.Fine	Ex.Fine	AU	Unc.	Proof
N46 ☐ 1894	5,413	10	14	20	40	75	160	235
N47 ☐ 1895	9,980	6	6	13	25	60	145	235
N48 ☐ 1896	8,843	8	8	16	35	62	150	235
N49 ☐ 1897	20,429	3	3	6	16	50	140	235
N50 ☐ 1898	12,532	4	3.50	7	18	52	145	235
N51 ☐ 1899	26,029	2.50	2	6	15	50	145	225
N52 ☐ 1900	27,256	2	2	5	15	40	135	225
N53 ☐ 1901	26,480	2	2	5	15	40	135	225
N54 ☐ 1902	31,490	2	2	5	15	40	135	225
N55 ☐ 1903	28,007	2	2	5	15	40	135	225
N56 ☐ 1904	21,405	2	2	5	15	40	135	225
N57 ☐ 1905	29,827	2	2	5	15	40	135	225
N58 ☐ 1906	38,614	2	2	5	15	40	135	225
N59 ☐ 1907	39,215	2	2	5	15	40	135	225
N60 ☐ 1908	22,686	2	2	5	15	40	135	225
N61 ☐ 1909	11,591	2	2.25	6	17	45	145	225
N62 ☐ 1910	30,169	2	2	5	15	40	135	225
N63 ☐ 1911	39,559	2	2	5	15	40	135	225
N64 ☐ 1912	26,237	2	2	5	15	40	135	225
N65 ☐ 1912D	8,474	4	3	8	40	90	250	
N66 ☐ 1912S	238	80	70	150	335	450	600	

N67 ☐ 1913* Not a regular issue - Extremely Rare.

*Only five pieces of this coin are known to exist. At one time four of them were in the possession of one collector. One sold in 1978 for $200,000, the other four are in museums.

NICKELS - INDIAN HEAD or Buffalo, 1913-1938

Denomination and date are the highest points of this coin, making it possible to find specimens in good state of preservation but lacking these details. Such pieces are only spending money. Early branch mint coins are seldom well struck and command substantial premiums when they are.

Mint Mark is on the Reverse. under "Five Cents"

1913-1938

1913-Type 1
Buffalo on High Mound

1913-Type 2
Buffalo on Level Ground

DATE	Mintages in 1000's	A.D.P. (VF)	Fine	V.Fine	Ex.Fine	AU	Unc.	Proof
N68 ☐ 1913 T-1	30,994	2	4	6	12	18	40	1,000
N69 ☐ 1913D T-1	5,337	5	9	11	20	36	65	
N70 ☐ 1913S T-1	2,105	12	10	23	36	55	100	
N71 ☐ 1913 T-2	29,859	3	5	7	12	23	40	1,200
N72 ☐ 1913D T-2	4,156	30	45	55	75	115	180	
N73 ☐ 1913S T-2	1,209	60	100	125	175	240	200	
N74 ☐ 1914	20,666	4	6	8	15	30	55	950
N75 ☐ 1914D	3,912	30	36	55	95	125	250	
N76 ☐ 1914S	3,470	6	9	15	32	48	110	
N77 ☐ 1915	20,987	3	4	6	12	25	50	1,100
N78 ☐ 1915D	7,569	15	12	30	50	65	150	
N79 ☐ 1915S	1,505	25	16	50	95	130	250	

	DATE	Mintages in 1000's	A.D.P. (VF)	Fine	V.Fine	Ex.Fine	AU	Unc.	Proof
N80	☐1916	63,498		1.50	2.50	5	15	40	1,250
N81	☐1916D	13,333	10	8	20	45	70	150	
N83	☐1916S	11,860	9	6	18	42	68	130	
N84	☐1917	51,424		1.75	3	10	25	45	
N85	☐1917D	9,911	20	11	36	75	110	220	
N86	☐1917S	4,193	15	10	32	65	100	235	
N87	☐1918	32,086	2	2	5	16	35	75	
N89	☐1918D	8,362	30	11	55	80	140	300	
N88	☐1918D Over 7		750	675	1,100	2,400	4,800	RARE	
N90	☐1918S	4,882	16	10	38	75	115	250	
N91	☐1919	60,868		1.25	3	7	20	40	
N93	☐1919D	8,006	30	13	60	100	150	350	
N94	☐1919S	7,521	20	7	40	75	110	275	
N95	☐1920	63,093		1.25	2.50	7	22	45	
N96	☐1920D	9,418	22	9	48	85	135	335	
N97	☐1920S	9,689	12	5	26	75	110	200	
N98	☐1921	10,683	3	2	.5	18	37	80	
N99	☐1921S	1,557	50	32	95	250	325	500	
N100	☐1923	35,175		1	2.25	6	15	35	
N101	☐1923S	6,142	8	4	20	50	75	160	
N102	☐1924	21,620		1	3	8	25	50	
N103	☐1924D	5,258	18	6	36	70	120	250	
N105	☐1924S	1,437	50	14	90	200	325	600	
N105	☐1925	35,565		1	2	6	19	35	
N106	☐1925D	4,450	20	10	46	75	125	300	
N107	☐1925S	6,256	9	5	20	44	85	225	
N108	☐1926	44,693		.75	1.50	5	15	32	
N109	☐1926D	5,638	20	8	47	80	120	150	
N110	☐1926S	970	22	11	60	180	320	500	

DATE	Mintages in 1000's	A.D.P. (EF)	E.Fine	Unc.	Unc.
N111 ☐ 1927	27,981	2	5	15	35
N112 ☐ 1927D	5,730	20	35	60	100
N113 ☐ 1927S	3,430	30	50	70	175
N114 ☐ 1928	23,411	1.50	4	16	35
N115 ☐ 1928D	6,436	6	11	25	50
N116 ☐ 1928S	6,936	4	9	30	70
N117 ☐ 1929	36,446	1.50	3.50	13	30
N118 ☐ 1929D	8,370	5	10	25	50
N119 ☐ 1929S	7,754	4	8	19	40
N120 ☐ 1930	22,849	1.50	3.50	15	30
N121 ☐ 1930S	5,435	2	7	23	55
N122 ☐ 1931S	1,200	5	10	25	60
N123 ☐ 1934	20,213	1	3	11	30
N124 ☐ 1934D	7,480	1	4	18	55
N125 ☐ 1935	58,264		2.50	8	16
N126 ☐ 1935D	12,092		4	18	50
N127 ☐ 1935S	10,300		3	12	30
N128 ☐ 1936*	119,001		2	7	14
N129 ☐ 1936D	24,418		3	9	18
N130 ☐ 1936S	14,390		3	11	20
N131 ☐ 1937*	79,486		2	7	12
N132 ☐ 1937D	17,826		2.50	8	13
N133 ☐ 1937D 3 Legged Buffalo		150	225	325	500
N134 ☐ 1937S	5,635		2.50	7.50	15
N135 ☐ 1938D	7,020		1.50	7	13
N136 ☐ 1938D Over S		4	8	15	25

Not usually collected in grades less than EF except for rare dates or mintmarks.

*Proofs 600

In 1938 the Treasury Department initiated a public competition for a new design for the nickel, stipulating that Thomas Jefferson be on the obverse and Monticello on the reverse. $1,000 was awarded to Felix Schlag for his design, and in 1966 his initials were engraved under Jefferson's shoulder. The Philadelphia mint mark appears on the wartime nickels minted 1942-1945.

Before 1968, the mint mark is on reverse to the right of building. This was changed in 1968 when the mint mark was placed on the obverse between the shoulder and the date. (On the wartime nickels the mint mark is larger and is placed over the dome of the building.)

1938
to date

1938-1942
1946-1968

1942-1945
Silver Content Type with
large mint mark over dome

DATE	Mintages in 1000's	A.D.P. (Unc.)	Unc.	Proof
N137 ☐ 1938	19,515		3	60
N138 ☐ 1938D	5,376	2	5	
N139 ☐ 1938S	4,105	3	6	
N140 ☐ 1939	120,628		2	45

Usually collected only in uncirculated and proof condition.

DATE	Mintages in 1000's	A.D.P. (Unc.)	Unc.	Proof
N142☐1939D	3,514	30	50	
N143☐1939S	6,630	20	30	
N144☐1940	176,499		1.50	35
N145☐1940D	43,540		2.50	
N146☐1940S	39,690		2.50	
N147☐1941	203,284		1	40
N148☐1941D	54,432		3.50	
N149☐1941S	43,445		5	
N150☐1942	49,819		2	40
N151☐1942D	13,938	8	30	
WARTIME SILVER NICKELS				
N153☐1942P	57,901	8	16	90
N154☐1942S	32,900	6	13	
N155☐1943P	271,176	2	3.75	
N156☐1943D	15,294	2	4	
N157☐1943S	104,060	2	4.50	
N158☐1944P	119,150	2	5	
N159☐1944D	32,309	5	10	
N160☐1944S	21,640	5	10	
N161☐1945P	119,408	3	7.50	
N163☐1945D	37,158	4	7	
N164☐1945S	58,939	2	3.50	

Usually collected only in uncirculated and proof condition. "Wartime" nickels contain 35% silver and, in used condition, will generally bring 4-5 times face value as melt coins.

NICKELS - JEFFERSON, 1946-1954

DATE	Mintages in 1000's	A.D.P. (Unc.)	Unc.	Proof
REGULAR PREWAR TYPE				
N165☐1946	161,116		.75	
N166☐1946D	45,292		1	
N167☐1946S	13,560		1	
N168☐1947	95,000		.75	
N169☐1947D	37,882		1	
N170☐1947S	24,720	1	1	
N171☐1948	89,348		.75	
N172☐1948D	44,734	.50	1.50	
N173☐1948S	11,300		1	
N174☐1949	60,652	.50	1.25	
N175☐1949D	36,498	.50	1.25	
N176☐1949S	9,716	1	2	
N177☐1950	9,847	.75	1.50	50
N178☐1950D	2,630	5	9	
N179☐1951	28,609		1	25
N180☐1951D	20,460		1	
N181☐1951S	7,776	1	2.50	
N182☐1952	64,070		.75	15
N183☐1952D	30,638	1	2	
N184☐1952S	20,572		.75	
N185☐1953	46,773			10
N186☐1953D	59,879			
N187☐1953S	19,211			
N188☐1954	47,917			5
N189☐1954D	117,183			
N190☐1954S	29,834			

Usually collected in uncirculated and proof condition.

NICKELS - JEFFERSON 1955 TO DATE

DATE	Mintages in 1000's	Unc.	Proof	DATE	Mintages in 1000's	Proof
N192☐1955	8,266	1	4	N221☐1970S	241,646	
N195☐1956	35,885		2	N224☐1971S*	3,224	2
N196☐1956D	67,223			N227☐1972S*	3,268	2
N197☐1957	39,656		2	N230☐1973S*	2,769	2
N198☐1957D	136,829			N233☐1974S*	2,617	5
N199☐1958	17,964		2			
N201☐1959	29,397		1			
N203☐1960	57,108		1	N236☐1975S*	2,909	4
N205☐1961	76,668		1	N239☐1976S*	4,150	2.
N206☐1961D	229,343			N242☐1977S*	3,251	3
N207☐1962	100,602		1			
N208☐1962D				N243☐1978	391,308	
N209☐1963	276,829			N244☐1978D	313,092	
N210☐1963D				N245☐1978S*	3,128	3
N211☐1964	1,028,623		1	N246☐1979	463,188	
N217☐1968S	103,438		1	N247☐1979D	325,867	
N219☐1969S	120,010		1	N248☐1979S*	3,677	2
				N249☐1980	593,004	
				1980D	502,323	
				1980S*	3,554	3.
				1981	657,504	
				1981D	364,801	
				1981S* TY1	4,063	1
				1981S* TY2		3
				1982		
				1982D		
				1982S*TY1.....		5
				1982S*TY2.....		2.50
				1983		
				1983D		

Unlisted coins command no premium at this writing.
*Issued in proof only

HALF DIMES - 1794-1873

Originally authorized in 1792, these coins were first minted in 1795, although the first examples are dated 1794. All the early issues up to 1805 are difficult to find in better than very fine condition.

LIBERTY WITH FLOWING HAIR 1794-1795

DATE	Mintages in 1000's	A.D.P. (F)	Good	V.Good	Fine	V.Fine	E.Fine
HD1☐1794.................	86	750	800	950	1,300	2,000	3,750
HD2☐1795.................		600	700	800	1,100	1,600	2,500

DRAPED BUST - SMALL EAGLE. 1796-1797

DATE	Mintages in 1000's	A.D.P. (F)	Good	V.Good	Fine	V.Fine	E.Fine
HD3☐1796 over 5		900	800	1,100	1,500	2,200	3,900
HD4☐1796.................	10	750	750	900	1,200	2,000	3,000
HD8☐1797 - 13 Stars		750	750	900	1,200	2,000	3,000
HD6☐1797 - 15 Stars	45	750	750	900	1,200	2,000	3,000
HD7☐1797 - 16 Stars		750	750	900	1,200	2,000	3,000

HALF DIMES - DRAPED BUST - LARGE OR HERALDIC EAGLE, 1800-05

DATE	Mintages in 1000's	A.D.P. (F)	Good	Fine	V.Fine	Ex.Fine	Unc.
HD9 □1800	24	500	575	900	1,250	2,300	9,500
HD10□1801	34	500	550	800	1,200	2,200	9,000
HD11□1802	13		2,300	7,250	12,000	24,000	—
HD12□1803 Sm.Dt.		500	575	750	1,250	2,300	9,500
HD13□1803 Lg.Dt.	38	500	575	750	1,250	2,300	9,500
HD14□1805	15	500	650	950	1,150	2,450	—

LIBERTY CAP. 1829-1837

DATE	Mintages in 1000's	A.D.P. (F)	Good	Fine	V.Fine	Ex.Fine	Unc.
HD15□1829	1,230	12	15	24	50	100	500
HD16□1830	1,240	12	15	24	50	100	450
HD18□1831	1,243	12	15	24	50	100	450
HD19□1832	965	12	15	24	50	100	500
HD20□1833	1,370	12	15	24	50	100	600
HD21□1834	1,480	12	15	24	50	100	450
HD22□1835	2,760	12	15	24	50	100	450
HD23□1836	1,900	12	15	24	50	100	450
HD24□1837 large 5c.		12	15	24	50	100	450
HD25□1837 small 5c.	2,270	30	25	60	95	200	525

HALF DIMES - LIBERTY SEATED 1837-1873

1837 AND 18380	1837-1859	1838-1839
no Stars		with Stars

(Mint Mark is on the reverse under the value)

DATE	Mintages in 1000's	A.D.P. (VF)	Good	Fine	V.Fine	Ex.Fine	Unc.
HD27□1837................		50	23	45	90	200	600
HD28□1838 0							
No Stars	70	100	50	100	200	450	4,000
STARS ADDED							
HD29□1838							
With Stars	2,250	8	6	10	18	50	350
HD31□1839................	1,069	8	6	10	18	50	350
HD32□1839 0	1,097	9	7	12	18	60	450
HD34□1849................	1,344	8	6	10	18	50	350
HD35□1840 0	935	8	7	10	18	65	600
DRAPERY ADDED FROM ELBOW TO KNEE							
HD37□1840................		9	6	12	25	70	800
HD38□1840 0		9	15	35	100	150	800
HD39□1841................	1,150	8	6	10	16	40	300
HD40□1841 0	815	9	7	10	20	55	700
HD41□1842................	815	8	6	10	16	40	300
HD42□1842 0	350	12	10	20	40	100	1,000
HD43□1843................	1,165	8	6	10	16	55	300
HD45□1844................	430	8	6	10	16	55	300

HALF DIMES - LIBERTY SEATED STARS OBVERSE
(ARROWS PLACED AT DATE 1853-1855 FOR REDUCED WEIGHT)

DATE	Mintages in 1000's	(VF)	Good	V.Good	Fine	V.Fine	Ex.Fine	Unc.	Proof
HD46 ☐ 1844 0	220	80	10	20	70	200	450	—	
HD48 ☐ 1845	1,564	10	6	8	12	18	40	300	
HD51 ☐ 1846	27	150	80	100	175	275	500	—	
HD52 ☐ 1847	1,274	10	6	8	12	18	40	300	
HD53 ☐ 1848	668	10	6	8	12	18	40	300	
HD55 ☐ 1848 0	600	15	10	15	30	50	80	700	
HD57 ☐ 1849	1,309	10	6	8	12	20	50	300	
HD56 ☐ 1849 Over 46		15	10	15	18	25	50	550	
HD58 ☐ 1849 Over 48		15	12	18	22	30	65	650	
HD59 ☐ 1849 0	140	85	25	40	65	160	300	—	
HD60 ☐ 1850	955	10	6	8	12	18	40	300	
HD61 ☐ 1850 0	690	15	10	15	20	35	50	700	
HD63 ☐ 1851	781	10	6	8	12	18	40	300	
HD64 ☐ 1851 0	860	15	10	15	20	35	50	600	
HD65 ☐ 1852	1,000	10	6	8	12	18	40	300	
HD66 ☐ 1852 0	260	35	20	30	50	70	125		
HD67 ☐ 1853 no arrows	135	25	13	20	30	40	80	600	
HD68 ☐ 1853 0 no arrows	160	175	100	125	200	300	600	—	
HD69 ☐ 1853 w/ arrows	13,210	8	6	9	12	16	42	325	
HD70 ☐ 1853 0 w/ arrows	2,200	8	6	9	12	16	42	350	
HD71 ☐ 1854 w/ arrows	5,740	8	6	3	12	16	42	325	
HD72 ☐ 1854 0 w/ arrows	1,560	15	6	9	12	30	60	750	
HD73 ☐ 1855 w/ arrows	1,750	8	6	8	12	16	40	325	1,700
HD74 ☐ 1855 0 w/ arrows	600	20	10	12	25	40	80	800	
HD75 ☐ 1856	4,880	8	6	8	10	16	40	650	1,500
HB76 ☐ 1856 0	1,100	10	6	8	12	18	42	725	
HD77 ☐ 1857	7,280	8	6	8	10	16	40	650	1,000
HD78 ☐ 1857 0	1,380	10	6	8	10	20	45	725	
HD79 ☐ 1858	3,500	8	6	8	10	16	40	650	800
HD82 ☐ 1858 0	1,600	10	6	8	10	20	45	725	
HD83 ☐ 1859	340	30	8	15	35	50	75	725	600
HD84 ☐ 1859 0	560	15	8	15	20	30	55	775	

HALF DIMES - LIBERTY SEATED
with "UNITED STATES OF AMERICA" on Obverse, 1860-1873

(Mint Marks are under or within wreath on Reverse)

Date	Mintages in 1000's	A.D.P. (VF)	Fine	V.Fine	Ex.Fine	AU	Unc.	Proof
HD87 ☐1860	799	8	10	14	30	65	275	325
HD88 ☐1860 0	1,060	8	12	15	32	70	300	
HD89 ☐1861	3,261	7	8	12	28	60	275	325
HD90 ☐1862	1,493	7	8	12	28	60	275	325
HD91 ☐1863	18	60	75	100	175	225	600	450
HD92 ☐1863S	100	25	27	42	95	250	700	
HD93 ☐1864	48	150	200	250	325	600	1,700	700
HD94 ☐1864S	90	40	50	70	125	600	1,300	
HD95 ☐1865	10	90	100	160	225	300	600	475
HD96 ☐1865S	120	30	30	55	85	250	800	
HD97 ☐1866	11	80	100	150	200	325	700	800
HD98 ☐1866S	120	25	27	45	100	325	750	
HD99 ☐1867	9	100	175	225	325	350	825	500
HD100☐1867S	120	35	30	60	100	375	750	
HD101☐1868	89	35	30	65	125	250	550	475
HD102☐1868S	280	12	15	20	40	175	325	
HD103☐1869	208	7	9	14	35	100	300	475
HD104☐1869S	230	7	10	14	35	100	350	
HD105☐1870	537	7	9	15	28	75	275	235
HD106☐1871	1,874	7	8	12	28	60	275	325
HD107☐1871S	161	35	40	65	100	170	475	
HD108☐1872	2,948	7	8	12	28	60	275	325
HD109☐1872S	837	8	10	15	30	70	300	
HD110☐1873	713	7	9	14	28	180	275	350
HD112☐1873S	324	8	10	15	30	70	300	

DIMES - 1796-TO DATE

DRAPED BUST, EAGLE ON REVERSE, 1796-1807

1796-1797
Small Eagle

1798-1807
Large Eagle

DATE	Mintages in 1000's	A.D.P. (F)	Good	V.Good	Fine	V.Fine	Ex.Fine	AU.	Unc.
D1 ☐1796	22	900	900	1,100	1,600	2,400	3,800	5,200	11,500
D2 ☐1797 16 stars.....	25	800	800	1,000	1,400	2,000	3,000	4,800	9,000
D3 ☐1797 13 stars.....		800	800	1,000	1,400	2,000	3,000	4,800	9,000
D5 ☐1798 Over 97 13 stars			700	1,250	2,300	6,000			
D4 ☐1798 Over 97 16 stars	27	250	475	600	800	1,000	1,450	2,500	4,200
D7 ☐1798		250	475	600	800	1,000	1,450	3,000	5,200
D8 ☐1800	22	250	475	600	800	1,000	1,450	3,000	4,200
D9 ☐1801	35	250	475	600	800	1,000	1,450	3,000	4,200
D10 ☐1802	11	250	475	600	800	1,000	1,450	3,000	4,200
D11 ☐1803	13	250	475	600	800	1,000	1,450	3,000	4,200
D13 ☐1804	8	350	500	700	1,000	2,000	3,250	4,400	6,200
D14 ☐1805	121	250	475	600	800	1,000	1,450	2,200	4,200
D16 ☐1807	165	250	475	600	800	1,000	1,450	2,200	4,200

DIMES - LIBERTY CAP, 1809-1837

DATE	Mintages in 1000's	A.D.P. (F)	Good	V.Good	Fine	V.Fine	Ex.Fine	AU	Unc.
D17 ☐ 1809	51	50	45	85	110	200	475	900	3,500
D18 ☐ 1811 Over 9	65	35	35	45	60	100	300	800	1,800
D20 ☐ 1814	421	16	15	20	30	90	300	750	1,700
D21 ☐ 1820	943	15	15	20	20	85	275	700	1,600
D24 ☐ 1821	1,187	15	15	18	24	85	275	700	1,500
D26 ☐ 1822	100	75	50	75	140	300	500	1,550	3,650
D27 ☐ 1823 Over 22	440	16	15	22	25	90	275	700	1,500
D30 ☐ 1824 Over 22		17	16	26	30	90	300	750	1,600
D31 ☐ 1825	510	13	15	18	24	85	275	700	1,500
D32 ☐ 1827	1,215	13	15	18	24	85	275	700	1,500
D33 ☐ 1828 Lg.Sz.		30	30	40	70	120	225	800	1,800
D34 ☐ 1828 Sm.Sz.		15	20	25	35	80	210	750	1,700
D36 ☐ 1829	770	11	12	14	22	50	180	425	1,200
D42 ☐ 1830	510	11	12	14	20	50	180	400	1,000
D43 ☐ 1831	771	11	12	14	20	50	180	400	1,000
D44 ☐ 1832	522	11	12	14	20	50	180	400	1,000
D45 ☐ 1833	485	11	12	14	20	50	180	400	1,000
D47 ☐ 1834	635	11	12	14	20	50	180	400	1,000
D48 ☐ 1835	1,410	11	12	14	20	50	180	400	1,000
D49 ☐ 1836	1,190	11	12	14	20	50	180	400	1,000
D50 ☐ 1837	1,042	11	12	14	20	50	180	400	1,000

DIMES - LIBERTY SEATED, 1837-1848

1837-38 O
no stars

1838-60
with stars

DATE	Mintages in 1000's	A.D.P. (F)	V.Good	Fine	V.Fine	Ex.Fine	AU	Unc.
D51 ☐ 1837 no stars		25	30	50	120	300	600	1,000
D53 ☐ 1838 O	406	50	80	100	180	400	1,800	3,500
D54 ☐ 1838 Sm.*	1,992	35	30	50	80	150	600	1,800
D55 ☐ 1838 Lg.		5	7	9	18	50	150	450
D56 ☐ 1839	1,053	5	6	9	18	50	150	400
D58 ☐ 1839 O	1,323	8	10	16	40	75	150	400
D59 ☐ 1840	1,359	6	6	12	20	60	150	400
D60 ☐ 1840 O	1,175	23	20	40	50	80	300	900
D61 ☐ 1840**	377	10	16	25	50	200	600	—
D63 ☐ 1841**	1,622	5	5	7	12	30	85	375
D65 ☐ 1841 O	2,007	16	15	30	40	65	375	900
D67 ☐ 1842	1,887	5	5	7	12	30	85	375
D68 ☐ 1842 O	2,020	5	5	7	12	40	110	5,000
D70 ☐ 1843	1,370	5	5	7	12	30	85	375
D72 ☐ 1843 O	150	35	30	70	250	750	2,000	—
D73 ☐ 1844	72	35	20	60	100	300	650	1,700
D74 ☐ 1845	1,755	5	5	7	12	30	100	400
D75 ☐ 1845 O	230	25	15	50	100	700	1,750	4,500
D76 ☐ 1846	31	55	50	100	175	400	1,100	8,000
D77 ☐ 1847	245	15	15	30	65	150	400	1,000
D78 ☐ 1848	451	5	5	8	18	35	110	400

*With stars on obverse.

**Drapery added to elbow, starting with 1840.

DIMES - LIBERTY SEATED, 1849-1860 (Cont'd.)

	DATE	Mintages in 1000's	A.D.P. (F)	Fine	V.Fine	Ex.Fine	AU	Unc.	Proof
D79	☐ 1849	839	5	10	20	30	85	425	
D80	☐ 1849-O	300	8	15	100	200	300	2,600	
D81	☐ 1850	1,931	4	8	15	30	100	400	
D82	☐ 1850-O	510	10	20	60	75	300	3,300	
D85	☐ 1851	1,026	4	8	15	35	100	400	
D86	☐ 1851-O	400	12	25	70	100	450	500	
D87	☐ 1852	1,535	4	8	15	35	100	400	
D88	☐ 1852-O	430	20	40	80	150	500	3,500	
D89	☐ 1853 No Arrows	95	25	50	100	200	400	1,200	
D90	☐ 1853 Arrows	12,078	4	8	15	40	100	450	7,000
D91	☐ 1853-O Arrows	1,100	5	10	30	100	300	1,500	
D92	☐ 1854 Arrows	4,470	4	8	15	40	100	400	
D93	☐ 1854-O Arrows	1,770	4	8	20	60	200	750	
D94	☐ 1855* Arrows	2,075	3	7	15	40	100	400	6,000
D95	☐ 1856*	5,780	3	6	12	30	85	350	1,700
D97	☐ 1856-O	1,180	3	6	12	45	175	500	
D101	☐ 1856S	70	35	65	150	250	250	2,800	
D102	☐ 1857	5,580	3	6	12	30	75	350	1,350
D103	☐ 1857-O	1,540	3	6	12	40	130	500	
D105	☐ 1858	1,540	3	6	12	30	75	350	1,000
D106	☐ 1858-O	290	6	12	40	100	200	1,800	
D107	☐ 1858S	60	28	60	150	300	500	2,000	
D108	☐ 1859*	430	4	9	20	50	150	500	700
D110	☐ 1859-O	480	3	6	25	60	140	600	
D112	☐ 1859S	60	35	70	160	325	600	—	
D113	☐ 1860S	140	25	35	70	150	250	800	

DIMES
LIBERTY SEATED with "UNITED STATES OF AMERICA"
on Obverse, 1860-1891

(Mint Marks are under or within Wreath on Reverse)

DATE	Mintages in 1000's	A.D.P. (F)	Fine	V.Fine	Ex.Fine	AU	Unc.	Proof
D114 ☐ 1860	607	4	7	10	20	50	200	500
D115 ☐ 1860-0	40	150	300	1,200	2,200	—		
D116 ☐ 1861	1,884	4	7	10	20	60	200	500
D117 ☐ 1861S	172	18	35	75	150	300	1,100	
D118 ☐ 1862	848	4	8	10	25	100	300	500
D119 ☐ 1862S	181	18	35	75	125	300	1,500	
D120 ☐ 1863	14	45	90	125	250	300	900	550
D121 ☐ 1863S	157	20	40	75	175	450	1,800	
D122 ☐ 1864	11	50	100	150	275	300	900	550
D123 ☐ 1864S	230	15	30	55	135	400	1,000	
D124 ☐ 1865	10	70	135	200	250	350	900	600
D125 ☐ 1865S	175	15	30	60	130	400	1,200	
D126 ☐ 1866	9	80	150	200	300	350	950	600
D127 ☐ 1866S	135	15	30	65	150	450	1,200	
D128 ☐ 1867	7	100	150	250	375	325	1,200	600
D129 ☐ 1867S	140	15	30	60	150	400	1,000	
D130 ☐ 1868	466	5	10	15	75	300	700	500
D131 ☐ 1868S	260	12	22	65	150	400	600	
D132 ☐ 1869	257	5	10	30	100	350	550	500
D133 ☐ 1869S	450	8	16	25	80	350	1,200	

DATE	Mintages in 1000's	A.D.P. (F) V.Good	Fine	V.Fine	Fine	AU	Unc.	Proof
D134 ☐1870*	471	8 6	8	20	40	100	450	575
D135 ☐1870S	50	65 70	130	175	300	500	3,600	
D136 ☐1871	907	3 4	6	9	30	50	400	575
D137 ☐1871S	320	16 15	30	55	125	200	500	
D138 ☐1871CC	20	375 450	600	1,000	1,900		—	
D139 ☐1872	2,396	3 4	6	10	30	50	200	575
D140 ☐1872S	190	20 20	40	95	175	400	1,500	
D141 ☐1872CC	32	125 200	300	450	975		—	
D142 ☐1873 closed 3 ...	1,508	3 4	6	9	30	60	200	600
D143 ☐1873 open 3	60	20 25	35	60	125	200	450	
D144 ☐1873CC	12	ONLY ONE KNOWN						
D145 ☐1873 w/arrows	2,378	10 10	20	35	100	250	800	900
D146 ☐1873S w/arrows	455	16 18	30	65	100	150	850	
D147 ☐1873CC w/arrows	19	275 400	600	1,000	2,000		—	
D148 ☐1874 w/arrows	2,941	10 10	20	35	100	250	800	900
D149 ☐1874S w/arrows	240	25 25	40	95	125	250	950	
D150 ☐1874CC w/arrows	11	750 500	1,000	1,700	3,000		—	
D151 ☐1875 no arrows	10,351	4	6	9	20	50	200	575
D153 ☐1875S	9,075	3 4	6	9	20	50	200	

DATE	Mintages in 1000's	A.D.P. (F)	Good	Fine	V.Fine	Ex.Fine	Unc.	Proof
D157 □ 1876	11,461	3	6	9	20	50	200	500
D159 □ 1876CC	8,270	4	7	17	20	50	225	
D158 □ 1876S	10,420	3	6	9	20	50	200	
D161 □ 1877	7,311	3	6	9	20	50	200	550
D163 □ 1877CC	7,700	3	6	9	20	50	250	
D162 □ 1877S	2,340	3	6	9	20	50	225	
D164 □ 1878	1,678	3	6	9	20	50	200	500
D165 □ 1878CC	200	18	35	60	125	250	500	
D166 □ 1879	15	37	65	120	175	275	550	550
D167 □ 1880	37	26	50	90	150	275	550	550
D168 □ 1881	25	26	50	100	150	275	550	550
D169 □ 1882	3,911	4	7	10	20	50	200	500
D170 □ 1883	7,676	3	6	9	20	50	200	500
D171 □ 1884	3,366	4	7	10	20	50	200	500
D172 □ 1884S	565	8	15	35	60	125	350	
D174 □ 1885	2,533	3	6	9	20	50	200	500
D175 □ 1885S	44	80	150	300	450	1,000	2,850	
D176 □ 1886	6,378	3	6	9	20	50	200	500
D177 □ 1886S	207	12	22	40	65	175	400	
D178 □ 1887	11,284	3	6	9	20	50	200	500
D179 □ 1887S	4,454	3	6	9	20	50	200	
D180 □ 1888	5,496	3	6	9	20	50	200	500
D181 □ 1888S	1,720	3	6	9	20	50	200	
D182 □ 1889	7,381	3	6	9	20	50	200	500
D183 □ 1889S	973	8	18	45	90	175	450	
D185 □ 1890	9,912	3	6	9	20	50	200	500
D186 □ 1890S	1,423	5	9	12	25	60	250	
D187 □ 1891	15,311	3	6	9	20	50	200	500
D188 □ 1891 0	4,540	3	6	9	20	50	200	
D189 □ 1891 S	3,196	3	6	9	20	50	200	

DIMES - LIBERTY HEAD OR "BARBER", 1892-1916

Named after Charles E. Barber who designed the coin. While Liberty is traditionally a woman on a coin, this one has a manly look. He used the same head on the obverse of the Barber quarter and half dollar.

(Mint Mark is under Wreath on the Reverse)

DATE	Mintages in 1000's	A.D.P. (VF)	Fine	V.Fine	Ex.Fine	Au	Unc.	Proof
D190 ☐ 1892	12,121	4	6	8	20	40	200	550
D191 ☐ 1892 O	3,842	8	8	15	30	55	300	
D192 ☐ 1892S	991	30	40	60	75	140	325	
D194 ☐ 1893	3,341	6	8	12	25	45	225	
D195 ☐ 1893 O	1,760	10	22	30	40	85	300	
D196 ☐ 1893S	2,491	8	11	18	30	60	250	
D197 ☐ 1894	1,331	10	12	25	50	95	260	550
D198 ☐ 1894 O	1,331	55	60	100	200	500	2,200	
D199 ☐ 1894S		PROOF ONLY						97,000
D200 ☐ 1895	691	45	75	95	150	275	550	650
D201 ☐ 1895 O	440	125	200	250	340	500	1,200	
D202 ☐ 1895S	1,120	20	25	35	45	80	300	
D203 ☐ 1896	2,001	8	10	16	35	55	200	550
D204 ☐ 1896 O	610	40	60	80	120	260	650	
D205 ☐ 1896S	575	35	52	70	105	210	450	
D206 ☐ 1897	10,869	3	3	6	16	35	150	550
D207 ☐ 1897 O	666	35	60	80	160	300	2,700	
D208 ☐ 1897S	1,343	15	16	30	50	85	350	
D209 ☐ 1898	16,321	3	3	6	16	35	150	550

DATE	Mintages in 1000's	A.D.P. (VF)	Fine	V.Fine	Ex.Fine	AU.	Unc.
D210 □ 1898 O	2,130	10	10	20	45	80	350
D211 □ 1898S	1,703	6	8	14	30	50	200
D212 □ 1899*	19,581	3	3	6	16	35	150
D213 □ 1899 O	2,650	10	9	22	45	75	350
D214 □ 1899S	1,867	7	8	15	30	50	250
D215 □ 1900*	17,601	3	3	6	16	35	150
D216 □ 1900 O	2,010	12	10	25	50	95	400
D217 □ 1900S	5,168	3	5	8	25	50	250
D218 □ 1901*	18,860	3	3	6	16	35	150
D219 □ 1901 O	5,620	6	5	13	40	95	300
D220 □ 1901S	593	50	70	100	180	350	600
D221 □ 1902*	21,381	3	3	6	16	35	150
D222 □ 1902 O	4,500	5	5	10	27	65	250
D223 □ 1902S	2,070	10	10	22	50	85	275
D224 □ 1903*	19,501	3	3	6	16	35	150
D225 □ 1903 O	8,180	4	4	8	25	60	250
D226 □ 1903S	613	35	45	70	120	250	700
D227 □ 1904*	14,601	3	3	6	16	35	150
D228 □ 1904S	800	30	35	60	110	225	600
D229 □ 1905*	14,552	3	5	6	16	35	150
D230 □ 1905 O	3,400	5	6	12	25	50	200
D232 □ 1905S	6,855	5	5	9	23	55	225
D233 □ 1906*	19,958	3	3	6	16	35	150
D234 □ 1906D	4,060	4	5	9	22	50	200
D235 □ 1906 O	2,610	8	8	15	27	55	220
D236 □ 1906S	3,137	4	5	10	25	55	225
D237 □ 1907*	22,221	3	3	6	16	35	150
D238 □ 1907D	4,080	5	5	9	25	55	220

*Proofs: 1899-1907 $300

For worn coins. see note at bottom of page 66.

DIMES - LIBERTY HEAD OR "BARBER" 1907-1916

DATE	Mintages in 1000's	A.D.P. (VF)	Fine	V.Fine	Ex.Fine	AU	Unc.
D239 ☐ 1907 0	5,058	4	5	9	25	55	225
D240 ☐ 1907S	3,178	5	6	10	25	60	240
D241 ☐ 1908*	10,601	3	3	6	16	35	150
D242 ☐ 1908D	7,490	4	4	7	18	40	200
D243 ☐ 1908 0	1,790	10	9	17	35	70	260
D244 ☐ 1908S	3,220	4	4	9	25	55	225
D245 ☐ 1909*	10,240	3	3	6	16	35	150
D246 ☐ 1909D	954	10	11	22	36	75	250
D247 ☐ 1909 0	2,287	6	6	12	26	55	220
D248 ☐ 1909S	1,000	10	10	22	37	80	300
D249 ☐ 1910*	11,521	4	3	6	16	35	150
D250 ☐ 1910D	3,490	4.50	4	10	30	70	250
D251 ☐ 1910S	1,240	6	8	15	28	65	240
D252 ☐ 1911*	18,871	3	3	6	16	35	150
D253 ☐ 1911D	11,209	3	4	6	16	35	150
D254 ☐ 1911S	3,520	3	4	7	18	45	200
D255 ☐ 1912*	19,351	3	3	6	16	35	150
D256 ☐ 1912D	11,760	3	4	6	16	35	150
D257 ☐ 1912S	3,420	3	4	8	22	55	200
D258 ☐ 1913*	19,761	3	3	6	16	35	150
D259 ☐ 1913S	510	22	22	45	85	160	375
D260 ☐ 1914*	17,361	3	3	6	16	35	150
D261 ☐ 1914D	11,908	3	4	6	16	35	150
D262 ☐ 1914S	2,100	4	5	8	22	55	250
D263 ☐ 1915*	5,620	4	3	6	16	35	150
D264 ☐ 1915S	960	5	5	10	28	70	240
D265 ☐ 1916	18,490	3	3	6	16	35	150
D266 ☐ 1916S	5,820	3	3	6	16	35	150

*Proofs: 1908-1915 $300

DIMES - MERCURY DIMES, 1916-1921

Called the Mercury dime, although the designer, A.A. Weinman intended that the wings added to Liberty's Cap should signify freedom of thought. The bundle of sticks on the reverse is called a "fasces", which, is the root from which the word "fascism" is derived. Thus, ironically, the mint unintentionally produced a coin which depicts the symbols of two diametrically opposed ideologies on obverse and reverse!

(Mint Mark is on Reverse at Bottom to Left of Branches)

DATE	Mintages in 1000's	A.D.P. (VF)	V.Fine	Ex.Fine	AU	Unc.
D267 ☐ 1916	22,180	3	6	9	15	22
D268 ☐ 1916D	264	525	1,050	1,325	1,800	2,175
D269 ☐ 1916S	10,450	4	8	14	21	33
D270 ☐ 1917	55,230			6	12	18
D271 ☐ 1917D	9,402	6	13	30	58	90
D272 ☐ 1917S	27,330	2	5	8	18	33
D273 ☐ 1918	26,680	4	9	20	35	51
D274 ☐ 1918D	22,675	4	8	18	36	60
D275 ☐ 1918S	19,300	3	2	11	22	39
D276 ☐ 1919	35,740	2	5	6	14	24
D277 ☐ 1919D	9,939	6	12	27	60	107
D278 ☐ 1919S	8,850	5	11	24	60	114
D279 ☐ 1920	59,030	2	4	6	12	18
D280 ☐ 1920D	19,171	3	6	12	28	60
D281 ☐ 1920S	13,820	2	5	11	22	55
D282 ☐ 1921	1,230	55	105	315	575	715

Collectable only in VF or better, except for rare dates and mintmarks, lesser grade common dates being saleable as silver bullion at about half the spot price for silver ounces per $1.00 face value. Uncirculated pieces with full split bands on the reverse command up to double the uncirculated price.

DIMES - MERCURY, 1921-1935 (Cont'd.)

DATE	Mintages in 1000's	A.D.P. (VF)	V.Fine	Ex.Fine	AU	Unc.
D283 ☐ 1921D	1,080	75	145	330	575	715
D284 ☐ 1923	50,130	2	4	6	10	17
D285 ☐ 1923S	6,440	3	7	16	35	66
D286 ☐ 1924	24,010	2	4	7	17	35
D287 ☐ 1924D	6,810	3	7	15	35	77
D288 ☐ 1924S	7,120	3	6	14	33	77
D289 ☐ 1925	25,610	2	4	6	15	31
D290 ☐ 1925D	5,117	8	20	55	108	205
D291 ☐ 1925S	5,850	3	6	15	39	88
D292 ☐ 1926	32,160	2	4	5	9	16
D293 ☐ 1926D	6,828	3	6	12	26	55
D294 ☐ 1926S	1,520	13	26	66	180	330
D295 ☐ 1927	28,080	2	4	5	9	16
D296 ☐ 1927D	4,812	5	10	28	66	143
D297 ☐ 1927S	4,770	2	5	11	29	66
D298 ☐ 1928	19,480	2	4	5	9	16
D299 ☐ 1928D	4,161	6	12	28	59	108
D300 ☐ 1928S	7,400	2	4	9	22	42
D301 ☐ 1929	25,970	1	3	4	7	12
D302 ☐ 1929D	5,034	3	6	8	17	35
D303 ☐ 1929S	4,730	2	4	5	12	36
D304 ☐ 1930	6,770	2	4	5	11	18
D305 ☐ 1930S	1,843	2	5	11	30	60
D306 ☐ 1931	3,150	2	4	8	16	30
D307 ☐ 1931D	1,260	7	15	26	48	99
D308 ☐ 1931S	1,800	2	5	10	30	60
D309 ☐ 1934	24,080				5	16
D310 ☐ 1934D	6,772	1	2	4	7	28
D311 ☐ 1935	58,830				5	11
D312 ☐ 1935D	10,477	1	2	7	10	36
D313 ☐ 1935S	15,840	1	2	5	8	21

DATE	Mintages in 1000's	A.D.P. (EF)	Ex.Fine	Unc.	Proof
D314 ☐ 1936	87,504			9	500
D315 ☐ 1936D	16,132			30	
D316 ☐ 1936S	9,210			20	
D317 ☐ 1937	58,866			9	300
D318 ☐ 1937D	14,146			30	
D319 ☐ 1937S	9,740			20	
D320 ☐ 1938	22,199			10	250
D321 ☐ 1938D	5,537			30	
D322 ☐ 1938S	8,090			20	
D323 ☐ 1939	67,749			7	175
D324 ☐ 1939D	24,394			7	
D325 ☐ 1939S	10,540			20	
D326 ☐ 1940	65,362			5	125
D327 ☐ 1940D	21,198			12	
D328 ☐ 1940S	21,560			6	
D329 ☐ 1941	175,107			12	125
D330 ☐ 1941D	45,634			20	
D331 ☐ 1941S	43,090			16	
D333 ☐ 1942	205,432			12	25
D332 ☐ 1942 Over 41		175	275	1,400	
D334 ☐ 1942D	60,740			18	
D335 ☐ 1942D Over 41		175	300	1,700	
D336 ☐ 1942S	49,300			24	
D337 ☐ 1943	191,710			12	
D338 ☐ 1943D	71,949			15	
D339 ☐ 1943S	60,400			20	
D340 ☐ 1944	321,410			12	
D341 ☐ 1944D	62,224			14	
D342 ☐ 1944S	49,490			14	
D343 ☐ 1945	159,130			12	
D344 ☐ 1945D	40,245			14	
D345 ☐ 1945S	41,920			14	

DIMES - ROOSEVELT, 1946 TO DATE

Issued as a memorial to Franklin D. Roosevelt, the denomination chosen as a tribute to the late President's affiliation with the March of Dimes.

(From 1968 Mint Mark at Base of Neck.)

DATE	Mintages in 1000's	A.D.P. (Unc.)	Unc.	Proof
D347 ☐ 1946	255,250	1	2	
D348 ☐ 1946D	61,043	2	3.50	
D349 ☐ 1946S	27,900	2	5	
D350 ☐ 1947	121,500	1	3	
D351 ☐ 1947D	46,835	3	6	
D352 ☐ 1947S	34,840	2	4	
D353 ☐ 1948	74,950	5	11	
D354 ☐ 1948D	52,841	5	9	
D355 ☐ 1948S	35,520	3	6	
D356 ☐ 1949	30,940	11	20	
D357 ☐ 1949D	26,034	5	10	
D358 ☐ 1949S	13,510	25	45	
D359 ☐ 1950	50,181	2	4	30
D360 ☐ 1950D	46,803	2	3.50	
D361 ☐ 1950S	20,440	12	20	
D362 ☐ 1951	103,938	2	2.50	25
D363 ☐ 1951D	56,529	2	2.50	
D364 ☐ 1951S	31,630	8	15	
D365 ☐ 1952	99,122	1	3	10
D366 ☐ 1952D	122,100	2	3.50	
D367 ☐ 1952S	44,419	3	6	
D368 ☐ 1953	53,619	1	2.50	10
D369 ☐ 1953D	136,433	1	2	
D370 ☐ 1953S	39,180	1	2	

DATE	Mintages in 1000's	Unc.	Proof
D371 ☐ 1954	114,244	2	4
D372 ☐ 1954D	106,397	2	
D373 ☐ 1954S	22,860	2	
D374 ☐ 1955	12,828	3	6
D375 ☐ 1955D	13,959	2	
D376 ☐ 1955S	18,510	2	
D377 ☐ 1956	109,309	2	2
D378 ☐ 1956D	108,015	2	
D379 ☐ 1957	161,408	2	2
D380 ☐ 1957D	113,354	2	
D381 ☐ 1958	32,786	2.25	2
D382 ☐ 1958D	136,565	2	
D383 ☐ 1959	86,929	2	1
D384 ☐ 1959D	164,920	2	
D385 ☐ 1960	72,082	2	1
D386 ☐ 1960D	200,160	2	
D387 ☐ 1961	96,758	2	1
D388 ☐ 1961D	209,147	2	
D389 ☐ 1962	75,668	2	1
D390 ☐ 1962D	334,948	2	
D391 ☐ 1963	126,726	2	1
D392 ☐ 1963D	421,477	2	
D393 ☐ 1964	933,311	2	1
D394 ☐ 1964D*	1,357,517	2	

END OF THE SILVER ISSUES

DATE	Mintages in 1000's	Unc.	Proof
D395 ☐ 1965	1,652,141		
D396 ☐ 1966	1,382,735		
D397 ☐ 1967	2,244,077		
D398 ☐ 1968	424,470		
D399 ☐ 1968D	480,748		
D400 ☐ 1968S	3,042	PROOF ONLY	1

*See note at bottom of page 66 for worn or common date coins.

DATE	Mintages in 1000's	Unc.	Proof	DATE	Mintages in 1000's	Unc.	Proof
D401☐1969	145,000			D416☐1974	470,248		
D402☐1969D	563,210			D417☐1974D	571,083		
D403☐1969S, Prf.Only	3,000		1	D418☐1974S Prf.Only	2,617		1
D404☐1970	345,570			D419☐1975	513,682		
D405☐1970D	754,942			D420☐1975D	313,705		
D406☐1970S Prf. Only	2,640		1	D421☐1975S Prf. Only	2,845		1
D407☐1971	162,690			D422☐1976	568,760		
D408☐1971D	377,914			D423☐1976D	695,223		
D409☐1971S Prf. Only	3,224		1	D424☐1976S Prf. Only	4,150		.75
D410☐1972	431,540			D425☐1977	796,930		
D411☐1972D	330,290			D426☐1977D	376,607		
D412☐1972S Prf. Only	3,268		1	D427☐1977S Prf. Only	3,251		.75
D413☐1973	315,670			D428☐1978	663,980		
D414☐1973D	455,032			D429☐1978D	282,847		
D415☐1973 Prf. Only	2,769		1	D430☐1978S Prf. Only	3,127		1
				D431☐1979	315,440		
				D432☐1979D	390,921		
				D432☐1979S TY1	3,677		1
				D433☐1979S TY2			3
				D434☐1980			
				D435☐1980D			
				D436☐1980S Prf. Only			1
				D437☐1981			
				D438☐1981D			
				D439☐1981S Prf. Only TY1			1
				D440☐1981S Prf. Only TY2			3
				D441☐1982			
				D442☐1982D			
				D443☐1982S Prf. Only			1.50

Issued at the behest of the old West which was experiencing a shortage of small change, the coin proved unpopular because of its similarity to the quarter.

DATE	Mintages in 1000's	A.D.P. [F]	Good	V.Good	Fine	V.Fine	Ex.Fine	AU	Unc.	Proof
DD1 ☐ 1875	40	40	40	50	70	100	180	400	1.400	1.000
DD3 ☐ 1875CC	133	40	40	50	65	100	170	375	1.300	
DD2 ☐ 1875S	1.155	35	35	40	60	90	160	350	1.000	
DD4 ☐ 1876	16	75	55	70	100	140	230	450	1.600	1.200
DD5 ☐ 1876CC	10								85.000	
DD6 ☐ 1877	(510)*									2.400
DD7 ☐ 1878	(600)*									1.800

QUARTERS - 1796 TO DATE

Quarters were seldom used in the early years. Consequently they were minted only in six years between 1796 and 1818 when a changing economy made them more useful. Only some 600,000 were produced in this period and all are scarce in high grades.

DRAPED BUST EAGLE. 1796-1807

1796
Small Eagle

1804-07
Large Eagle

	DATE	Mintages in 1000's	A.D.P. (F)	Good	V. Good	Fine	V. Fine	Ex. Fine	AU	Unc.
Q1	☐1796	6	2,000	2,550	3,100	3,550	6,300	9,650	14,000	20,000
Q2	☐1804	7	700	600	1,000	1,400	2,400	6,400	16,000	20,000
Q3	☐1805	121	225	205	265	440	840	1,450	2,550	6,000
Q7	☐1806	206	225	205	265	440	840	1,450	2,550	6,000
Q6	☐1806 over 5		225	205	265	440	840	1,450	2,550	6,000
Q8	☐1807	221	225	205	265	440	840	1,450	2,550	6,000

QUARTERS - CAPPED BUST, 1815-1838

1815-1838

1815-28 Motto over Eagle

1831-38
Without Motto—
reduced size

	DATE	Mintages in 1000's	A.D.P. (F)	Good	V. Good	Fine	V. Fine	Ex. Fine	AU	Unc.
Q9	☐ 1815	89	40	44	51	77	205	500	1,150	1,500
Q11	☐ 1818	361	40	44	51	77	205	510	1,150	1,500
Q10	☐ 1818 Over 15		50	55	62	90	215	525	1,300	1,750
Q12	☐ 1819*	144	40	44	51	77	205	510	1,150	1,500
Q14	☐ 1820†	127	40	44	51	77	205	510	1,150	1,500
Q16	☐ 1821	217	40	44	51	77	205	510	1,150	1,500
Q17	☐ 1822	64	40	44	51	77	205	510	1,150	1,500
Q18	☐ 1822 25 Over 50c		225	225	325	425	775	1,300	1,750	3,750
Q19	☐ 1823 Over 22	18	6,000	2,500	5,500	12,500	15,000	19,000	RARE	RARE
Q20	☐ 1824		40	44	51	77	205	510	1,150	1,500
Q22	☐ 1825 Over dates	168	40	44	51	77	205	510	1,150	1,500
Q24	☐ 1827 Orig.	4	1980 Auction				Proof 190,000			
Q25	☐ 1827 Restrike						Proof 23,500			
Q26	☐ 1828		40	44	50	77	205	510	1,150	1,500
Q27	☐ 1828 25 Over 50c	102	100	75	125	250	425	725	1,900	3,000
	REDUCED SIZE — NO MOTTO OVER EAGLE ON REVERSE									
Q28	☐ 1831	398	24	32	38	48	99	265	630	900
Q33	☐ 1832	320	24	32	38	48	99	265	630	900
Q34	☐ 1833	156	24	32	38	48	99	265	630	900
Q36	☐ 1834	286	24	32	38	48	99	265	630	900
Q37	☐ 1835	1,952	24	32	38	48	99	265	630	900
Q39	☐ 1836	472	24	32	38	48	99	265	630	900
Q40	☐ 1837	252	24	32	38	48	99	265	630	900
Q41	☐ 1838 both types.	832	24	32	38	48	99	265	630	900

*Small and large 9   †Small and large 0   ††Original   Proof: Q19, $32,000 (1977)

QUARTERS - LIBERTY SEATED 1838-1891
NO MOTTO ABOVE EAGLE 1838-1865

Mint Mark

1838-1865

DATE	Mintages in 1000's	A.D.P. (F)	V.Good	Fine	V.Fine	Ex.Fine	AU	Unc.
Q42 ☐1838 No Drapery		6	10	12	47	170	400	1,500
Q43 ☐1839 No Drapery	491	6	10	12	47	170	400	1,500
Q44 ☐1840 0 No Drapery	425	6	10	12	47	170	400	1,500
Q45 ☐1840	188	40	40	75	175	350	600	2,400
Q46 ☐1840 0		40	40	75	125	225	450	1,500
Q47 ☐1841	120	80	100	150	200	400	500	1,000
Q48 ☐1841 0	452	40	40	75	100	200	300	1,000
Q50 ☐1842	88	100	150	200	250	425	650	2,700
Q51 ☐1842 0 Sm.Dt.....		350	500	700	1,000	2,000	RARE	RARE
Q52 ☐1842 0 Lg.Dt.....		25	30	45	75	175	500	RARE
Q53 ☐1843	46	6	7	11	21	48	105	375
Q54 ☐1843 0	968	25	30	45	70	175	500	RARE
Q56 ☐1844	421	6	7	11	21	48	105	375
Q57 ☐1844 0	740	6	7	11	21	48	275	1,100
Q58 ☐1845	922	6	7	11	21	48	105	375
Q59 ☐1846	510	6	7	11	21	48	105	375
Q60 ☐1847	734	6	7	11	21	48	105	375
Q61 ☐1847 0	368	35	45	70	175	275	375	725
Q62 ☐1848	340	60	75	120	190	350	450	725
Q64 ☐1849	340	10	35	60	90	175	275	600
Q65 ☐1849 0		450	450	600	900	2,000	RARE	RARE

1842 Sm.Dt. Proof 1978 Auction 32,500.

DATE	Mintages in 1000's	A.D.P. (F)	V. Good	Fine	V. Fine	Ex. Fine	AU	Unc.	Proof
Q66 ☐ 1850	191	45	60	90	100	200	325	1,000	
Q67 ☐ 1850 0	412	40	50	75	100	200	325	1,100	
Q68 ☐ 1851	160	50	75	100	125	250	350	1,000	
Q69 ☐ 1851 0	88	200	225	400	600	1,200	3,000	RARE	
Q70 ☐ 1852	177	50	75	100	125	250	350	900	
Q71 ☐ 1852 0	96	250	375	475	700	1,300	3,000	RARE	
Q72 ☐ 1853	44	200	300	400	500	700	1,250	4,250	
Q73 ☐ 1853 ARROWS & RAYS	15,254	8	8	15	36	110	300	875	
Q74 ☐ 1853 0 ARROWS & RAYS	1,332	22	30	45	80	200	450	2,750	
Q75 ☐ 1854 ARROWS	12,380	6	7	12	24	66	200	690	
Q76 ☐ 1854 0 ARROWS	1,484	15	20	30	50	125	200	2,400	
Q79 ☐ 1855 ARROWS	2,857	6	7	12	24	66	200	690	1,100
Q80 ☐ 1855 0 ARROWS	1,484	40	50	75	125	325	475	1,850	
Q81 ☐ 1855 S ARROWS	396	40	35	75	125	300	450	1,750	
Q82 ☐ 1856	7,264	6	7	11	21	48	105	375	1,200
Q83 ☐ 1856 0	968	20	14	40	55	125	250	825	
Q84 ☐ 1856 S	286	40	50	75	150	275	500	RARE	
Q86 ☐ 1857	9,644	6	7	11	21	48	105	375	1,200
Q87 ☐ 1857 0	1,180	10	14	20	30	60	175	900	
Q88 ☐ 1857 S	82	90	75	175	250	500	850	RARE	
Q89 ☐ 1858	7,368	6	7	11	21	48	105	375	875
Q90 ☐ 1858 0	520	20	25	40	55	125	250	900	
Q91 ☐ 1858 S	121	75	35	150	225	425	800	RARE	
Q92 ☐ 1859	1,344	6	7	11	21	48	105	900	750
Q93 ☐ 1859 0	260	40	50	75	110	200	350	900	
Q94 ☐ 1859 S	80	75	75	150	250	475	1,500	RARE	
Q95 ☐ 1860	805	6	7	11	21	48	105	900	425
Q96 ☐ 1860 0	388	22	30	45	70	150	250	925	
Q97 ☐ 1860 S	56	120	125	225	400	600	2,000	RARE	
Q98 ☐ 1861	4,854	6	7	11	21	48	105	375	425

QUARTERS - LIBERTY SEATED, 1861-1865

	DATE	Mintages in 1000's	A.D.P. (F)	V.Good	Fine	V.Fine	Ex.Fine	AU	Unc.	Proof
Q99	☐1861S	96	75	50	150	225	300	550	2,600	
Q100	☐1862	933	6	7	11	21	48	105	375	425
Q101	☐1862S	67	90	75	175	275	375	750	RARE	—
Q102	☐1863	192	20	30	40	75	150	225	750	475
Q103	☐1864	94	50	75	100	175	300	450	900	675
Q104	☐1864S	20	175	200	350	500	1,000	1,250	1,800	
Q105	☐1865	59	50	75	100	175	300	400	1,250	750
Q106	☐1865S	41	90	90	180	275	425	650	2,000	
Q107	☐1866	UNIQUE								

QUARTERS
LIBERTY SEATED, MOTTO ABOVE EAGLE, 1866-1891

	DATE	Mintages in 1000's	A.D.P. (F)	V.Good	Fine	V.Fine	Ex.Fine	AU	Unc.	Proof
Q108	☐1866	18	160	250	325	450	700	900	1,400	1,000
Q109	☐1866S	28	160	175	325	475	750	950	RARE	
Q110	☐1867	21	100	125	200	250	450	700	1,300	1,000
Q111	☐1867S	48	75	75	150	250	425	575	3,000	
Q112	☐1868	30	90	110	175	250	350	500	1,200	1,000
Q113	☐1868S	96	32	30	65	125	200	350	2,300	
Q114	☐1869	17	140	200	275	375	700	900	1,400	1,000
Q115	☐1869S	76	35	150	225	350	450	600	RARE	
Q116	☐1870	87	50	50	100	175	250	450	1,000	600

QUARTERS - LIBERTY SEATED, MOTTO OVER EAGLE 1870-1873

DATE	Mintages in 1000's	(F) V.Good	Fine	V.Fine	Ex.Fine	AU	Unc.	Proof
Q177 ☐ 1870CC	8	1,100 1,250	2,250	2,750	3,750	RARE	RARE	
Q118 ☐ 1871	120	15 20	30	60	125	275	1,000	600
Q120 ☐ 1871CC	11	550 650	1,100	1,800	2,800	4,000	RARE	
Q119 ☐ 1871S	31	145 250	425	525	800	1,000	3,000	
Q121 ☐ 1872	183	12 10	25	50	100	250	1,000	600
Q122 ☐ 1872CC	9	225 325	450	700	1,800	RARE	RARE	
Q123 ☐ 1872S	83	165 250	350	425	700	1,500	4,700	
Q124 ☐ 1873 No Arrows	213	25 30	50	100	175	250	550	600
Q126 ☐ 1873CC No Arrows	4	1980 Auction 205,000						
Q127 ☐ 1873 w/arrows....	1,264	11 12	21	53	150	325	875	770
Q128 ☐ 1873S w/arrows...	156	11 12	21	53	150	325	875	
Q129 ☐ 1873CC w/arrows	12	375 500	750	1,400	2,250	RARE	RARE	

ARROWS ADDED 1873-1874

Q130 ☐ 1884* w/arrows..	472	11 12	21	53	150	325	875	770
Q131 ☐ 1874S* w/arrows.	392	11 12	21	53	150	325	875	
Q132 ☐ 1875	4,293	5 7	10	18	46	99	325	385
Q136 ☐ 1875CC	140	50 50	100	200	350	500	1,400	

QUARTERS - LIBERTY SEATED
MOTTO OVER EAGLE 1875-1891

DATE	Mintages in 1000's	A.D.P. (F)	V.Good	Fine	V.Fine	Ex.Fine	AU	Unc.	Proof
Q133 ☐1875S	680	13	14	24	50	90	250	325	
Q137 ☐1876	17,817	5	7	10	18	46	99	325	385
Q138 ☐1876CC	8,596	5	7	10	18	46	99	325	
Q140 ☐1876S	4,944	5	7	10	18	46	99	325	
Q142 ☐1877	10,912	5	7	10	18	46	99	325	385
Q146 ☐1877CC	4,192	5	7	10	18	46	99	800	
Q143 ☐1877S	8,996	5	7	10	18	46	99	325	
Q147 ☐1878	2,261	10	15	20	35	65	110	325	385
Q149 ☐1878CC	996	23	30	45	75	125	175	325	
Q148 ☐1878S	140	45	50	85	125	225	650	1,500	
Q150 ☐1879	15	75	100	150	225	300	350	440	600
Q151 ☐1880	15	75	100	150	225	300	350	440	600
Q152 ☐1881	13	75	125	150	225	300	350	440	600
Q153 ☐1882	16	75	125	150	225	300	350	440	600
Q154 ☐1883	15	75	125	150	225	300	350	440	600
Q155 ☐1884	9	75	125	150	225	300	350	440	600
Q156 ☐1885	15	75	125	150	225	300	350	440	600
Q157 ☐1886	6	150	250	300	350	400	500	650	600
Q158 ☐1887	11	75	125	150	225	300	350	440	600
Q159 ☐1888	11	75	125	150	225	300	350	440	600
Q160 ☐1888S	1,216	5	7	10	18	99	325		
Q161 ☐1889	13	75	125	150	225	300	350	440	600
Q162 ☐1890	81	40	55	75	90	175	300	900	600
Q163 ☐1891	3,921	5	7	10	18	46	99	325	600
Q164 ☐1891 0	68	110	140	220	400	600	RARE	RARE	
Q165 ☐1891S	2,216	5	7	10	18	46	99	325	

QUARTERS - LIBERTY HEAD OR BARBER, 1892-1916

Long considered one of our most beautiful coins, these are identical to both the dime and half dollar, all of which were designed by Charles E. Barber.

Mint Mark is below
the eagle on Reverse

DATE	Mintages in 1000's	A.D.P. (VF)	Fine	V.Fine	Ex.Fine	AU	Unc.	Proof
Q166 ☐ 1892	8,327	8	10	16	42	109	265	360
Q168 ☐ 1892 0	2,640	10	11	20	52	132	290	
Q170 ☐ 1892S	964	21	26	41	76	182	350	
Q172 ☐ 1893	5,445	8	10	16	44	96	265	360
Q173 ☐ 1893 0	3,396	10	11	20	52	132	300	
Q174 ☐ 1893S	1,455	14	13	27	58	143	300	
Q175 ☐ 1894	3,433	9	10	18	44	96	265	360
Q176 ☐ 1894 0	2,895	10	11	20	54	137	300	
Q177 ☐ 1894S	2,649	10	11	20	54	137	300	
Q178 ☐ 1895	4,441	8	10	16	44	96	270	360
Q179 ☐ 1895 0	2,816	10	10	20	55	155	350	
Q180 ☐ 1895S	1,765	13	13	26	54	143	315	
Q181 ☐ 1896	3,875	10	9	20	46	102	270	360
Q182 ☐ 1896 0	1,484	18	14	35	99	355	690	
Q183 ☐ 1896S	188	450	525	890	1,485	2,200	3,000	
Q184 ☐ 1897	8,141	8	8	15	36	92	265	360
Q185 ☐ 1897 0	1,415	20	15	40	102	380	715	
Q186 ☐ 1897S	542	20	20	40	88	220	330	
Q187 ☐ 1898	11,101	8	8	15	36	92	265	360

DATE	Mintages in 1000's	A.D.P. (VF)	Fine	V.Fine	Ex.Fine	AU	Unc.	Proof
Q188 ☐ 1898	1,868	12	12	24	60	200	420	
Q189 ☐ 1898S	1,021	10	10	21	48	165	330	
Q190 ☐ 1899	12,625	8	8	15	36	92	265	360
Q191 ☐ 1899 O	2,644	12	12	23	55	195	360	
Q192 ☐ 1899S	708	15	15	30	60	175	330	
Q193 ☐ 1900	10,017	8	8	15	36	92	265	360
Q194 ☐ 1900 O	3,416	14	13	28	66	205	375	
Q195 ☐ 1900S	1,859	10	11	21	48	132	300	
Q196 ☐ 1901	8,893	8	8	15	36	92	225	360
Q197 ☐ 1901 O	1,612	28	28	55	120	360	690	
Q198 ☐ 1901S	73	875	1,735	2,400	3,400	5,250	15,000	
Q199 ☐ 1902	12,198	8	8	15	36	92	265	360
Q200 ☐ 1902 O	4,748	10	11	21	51	150	350	
Q201 ☐ 1902S	1,525	15	14	29	72	175	335	
Q202 ☐ 1903	9,670	8	8	15	36	92	265	360
Q203 ☐ 1903 O	3,500	12	11	24	55	138	300	
Q204 ☐ 1903S	1,036	15	14	30	76	195	350	
Q205 ☐ 1904	9,589	8	8	15	36	92	265	360
Q206 ☐ 1904 O	2,456	16	14	32	90	355	635	
Q207 ☐ 1905	4,968	8	8	15	36	92	245	360
Q208 ☐ 1905 O	1,230	14	14	27	54	132	320	
Q209 ☐ 1905S	1,884	12	12	23	47	127	305	
Q210 ☐ 1906	3,656	8	8	15	36	92	265	360
Q211 ☐ 1906D	3,280	9	9	18	42	108	280	
Q212 ☐ 1906 O	2,056	10	11	20	44	108	280	
Q213 ☐ 1907	7,193	8	8	15	36	92	265	360
Q214 ☐ 1907D	2,484	9	9	18	42	110	290	
Q215 ☐ 1907 O	4,560	8	9	16	40	102	275	

Coins below the grade of fine, except for rarities can usually be sold as melt silver at about ½ the spot price for silver ounce per $1.00 face.

Date	Mintages in 1000's	A.D.P. (F)	Good	Fine	V.Fine	Ex.Fine	Unc.	Proof
Q216 ☐ 1907S	1.350	9	10	18	48	120	325	
Q217 ☐ 1908	4.233	8	8	15	36	92	265	360
Q218 ☐ 1908D	5.788	8	8	16	40	102	275	
Q219 ☐ 1908 O	6.244	8	8	16	40	102	265	
Q220 ☐ 1908S	784	15	16	30	72	174	350	
Q221 ☐ 1909	9.269	8	8	15	36	92	265	360
Q222 ☐ 1909D	5.114	8	8	16	40	102	275	
Q223 ☐ 1909 O	712	26	28	52	127	275	515	
Q224 ☐ 1909S	1.348	9	8	17	42	132	330	
Q225 ☐ 1910	2.245	8	8	15	36	92	265	360
Q226 ☐ 1901D	1.500	9	9	18	44	114	300	
Q227 ☐ 1911	3.271	8	8	15	36	92	265	360
Q228 ☐ 1911D	934	10	10	19	44	96	275	
Q229 ☐ 1911S	988	9	9	18	46	114	315	
Q230 ☐ 1912	4.401	8	8	15	36	92	265	360
Q231 ☐ 1912S	708	10	9	19	48	120	330	
Q232 ☐ 1913	485	51	39	102	330	525	1.075	900
Q233 ☐ 1913D	1.451	10	8	19	44	108	275	
Q234 ☐ 1913S	40	375	540	845	1.430	3.100	3.000	
Q235 ☐ 1914	6.245	8	8	15	36	92	265	360
Q236 ☐ 1914D	3.046	9	8	17	36	91	265	
Q237 ☐ 1914S	264	45	33	90	200	358	600	
Q238 ☐ 1915	3.480	8	8	15	36	92	265	360
Q239 ☐ 1915D	3.694	8	8	15	36	92	265	
Q240 ☐ 1915S	704	11	11	21	44	102	280	
Q241 ☐ 1916	1.788	8	8	15	36	92	265	360
Q242 ☐ 1916D	6.541	8	8	15	36	92	265	

QUARTERS - STANDING LIBERTY. 1916-1930

Fitting his design to the mood of the country on our impending entrance into WWI, Herman A. McNeil designed this quarter depicting an armed and ready Liberty, (with mail and shield) but one which was ready to accept peace (with an olive branch). The first issues showed Liberty partially exposed, which, due to public modesty was corrected in 1917. The date in the first type was too high, and wore poorly. This, too, was corrected in 1917. Coins with full Liberty head are worth about double prices shown.

TYPE I   TYPE II

Mint Mark is to
left of Date on Obverse

1916-1917
No Stars
under Eagle

1917-1930
3 Stars Under Eagle

DATE	Mintages in 1000's	A.D.P. (VF)	Fine	V.Fine	Ex.Fine	AU	Unc.
0243 ☐ 1916	52	925	1.485	1.800	2.290	2.650	3.300
0244 ☐ 1917	8.792	13	12	27	52	96	132
0245 ☐ 1917D	1.509	24	22	48	84	114	156
0246 ☐ 1917S	1.952	22	19	44	77	120	168
STARS UNDER EAGLE—TYPE II							
0247 ☐ 1917	13.880	11	16	22	36	60	102
0248 ☐ 1917D	6.224	27	42	54	84	114	151
0249 ☐ 1917S	5.552	24	29	48	70	96	138
0250 ☐ 1918	14.240	15	21	30	44	72	132

See note at bottom of page 82 for worn coins.

DATE	Mintages in 1000's	A.D.P. (F)	V.Fine	Ex.Fine	AU	Unc.
Q251 □ 1918D	7,380	26	52	77	120	193
Q252 □ 1918S	11,072	12	24	42	72	132
Q253 □ 1918S over 17	1,100	2,175	3,525	5,250	7,900
Q254 □ 1919	11,324	23	46	60	84	132
Q255 □ 1919D	1,944	64	127	204	270	451
Q256 □ 1919S	1,836	53	105	180	240	385
Q257 □ 1920	27,860	10	20	33	58	107
Q258 □ 1920D	3,586	35	69	96	143	198
Q259 □ 1920S	6,380	13	26	44	72	132
Q260 □ 1921	1,916	72	143	204	289	385
Q261 □ 1923	9,716	11	22	36	60	114
Q262 □ 1923S	1,360	110	220	330	418	512
Q263 □ 1924	10,920	11	22	36	60	114
Q264 □ 1924D	3,112	29	58	83	102	132
Q265 □ 1924S	2,860	12	24	40	69	132
Q266 □ 1925	12,280	7	13	24	51	102
Q267 □ 1926	11,316	7	13	24	51	102
Q268 □ 1926D	1,716	10	19	40	72	102
Q269 □ 1926S	2,700	10	19	48	92	157
Q270 □ 1927	11,912	7	13	24	51	102
Q271 □ 1927D	976	12	24	51	82	132
Q272 □ 1927S	396	60	120	440	842	1,375
Q273 □ 1928	6,336	7	13	24	51	102
Q274 □ 1928D	1,628	9	17	33	64	120
Q275 □ 1928S	2,644	7	14	28	55	108
Q276 □ 1929	11,140	7	13	24	51	96
Q277 □ 1929D	1,358	7	15	30	60	113
Q278 □ 1929S	1,764	7	14	26	53	96
Q279 □ 1930	5,632	7	14	24	51	96
Q280 □ 1930S	1,556	7	14	26	53	96

Issued to commemorate the 200th birthday of George Washington, this quarter, designed by John Flanagan, proved so popular that it was adopted for general circulation.

1932-67 Mint Mark is on Reverse Below Eagle   1968 on—Mint Mark to Right of Hair Ribbon

DATE	Mintages in 1000's	A.D.P. (EF)	Ex.Fine	AU	Unc.	Proof
Q281 □ 1932	5.404	5	10	14	27	
Q282 □ 1932D	437	87	173	268	480	
Q283 □ 1932S	408	45	90	143	230	
Q284 □ 1934	31.912	4	8	13	45	
Q288 □ 1934D	3.537	9	18	41	90	
Q289 □ 1935	32.484	4	8	13	30	
Q290 □ 1935D	5.780	9	17	39	90	
Q291 □ 1935S	5.660	5	11	24	66	
Q292 □ 1936	41.304	4	8	13	30	750
Q293 □ 1936D	5.374	15	29	82	162	
Q295 □ 1936S	3.828	5	11	27	66	
Q296 □ 1937	19.702	4	8	13	30	165
Q297 □ 1937D	7.190	5	10	18	32	
Q298 □ 1937S	1.652	9	17	44	88	

For worn coins see note at bottom of page 82.

DATE	Mintages in 1000's	A.D.P. (EF)	Ex.Fine	AU	Unc.	Proof
Q299 ☐ 1938	9,480	7	14	26	53	150
Q300 ☐ 1938S	2,832	5	10	21	44	
Q301 ☐ 1939	33,549		5	10	18	75
Q302 ☐ 1939D	7,092	4	8	14	24	
Q303 ☐ 1939S	2,628	5	11	24	46	
Q304 ☐ 1940	35,715		5	10	16	65
Q305 ☐ 1940D	2,798	5	12	28	55	
Q306 ☐ 1940S	8,244	4	9	13	20	
Q307 ☐ 1941	79,047		4	5	9	60
Q308 ☐ 1941D	16,715	4	9	13	22	
Q309 ☐ 1941S	16,080	4	9	13	22	
Q310 ☐ 1942	102,117		2	3	7	60
Q311 ☐ 1942D	17,487		3	6	13	
Q312 ☐ 1942S	19,384	3	6	15	60	
Q313 ☐ 1943	99,700		2	3	9	
Q314 ☐ 1943D	16,096		4	8	15	
Q315 ☐ 1943S	21,700		3	8	37	
Q316 ☐ 1944	104,956		2	3	5	
Q317 ☐ 1944D	14,600		2	4	12	
Q318 ☐ 1944S	12,560	2	4	6	12	
Q319 ☐ 1945	74,372		2	3	6	
Q320 ☐ 1945D	12,342		2	3	9	
Q321 ☐ 1945S	17,007		2	3	7	
Q322 ☐ 1946	53,436			2	4	
Q323 ☐ 1946D	9,073		2	3	5	
Q324 ☐ 1946S	4,204		2	3	6	

See note at bottom of page 82.

DATE	Mintages in 1000's	A.D.P. (Unc.)	Unc.	Proof
Q325 ☐ 1947	22,556	3	7	
Q326 ☐ 1947D	15,338	3	7	
Q327 ☐ 1947S	5,532	3	6	
Q328 ☐ 1948	35,196	2	4	
Q329 ☐ 1948D	16,767	3	6	
Q330 ☐ 1948S	15,960	4	7	
Q331 ☐ 1949	9,312	10	20	
Q332 ☐ 1949D	10,068	5	10	
Q333 ☐ 1950	24,972	2	4	70
Q334 ☐ 1950D	21,076	2	4	
Q335 ☐ 1950S	10,284	3	7	
Q336 ☐ 1951	43,506	2	4	40
Q337 ☐ 1951D	35,355	2	4	
Q338 ☐ 1951S	8,948	4	9	
Q339 ☐ 1952	38,862	2	4	25
Q340 ☐ 1952D	49,795	2	4	
Q341 ☐ 1952S	13,708	3	6	
Q342 ☐ 1953	18,665	2	4	14
Q343 ☐ 1953D	56,112		3	
Q344 ☐ 1953S	14,016	2	4	
Q345 ☐ 1954	54,646		3	10
Q346 ☐ 1954D	46,305		3	
Q347 ☐ 1954S	11,835		3	
Q348 ☐ 1955	18,558		3	8
Q349 ☐ 1955D	3,182	2	4	
Q350 ☐ 1956	44,813		3	4
Q351 ☐ 1956D	32,334		3	

See note at bottom of page 82.

DATE	Mintages in 1000's	Unc.	Proof
Q352 □ 1957	47,780	3	4
Q353 □ 1957D	77,924	3	
Q354 □ 1958	7,236	3	4
Q355 □ 1958D	78,125	3	
Q356 □ 1959	25,533	3	4
Q357 □ 1959D	62,054	3	
Q358 □ 1960	30,856	3	
Q359 □ 1960D	63,000	3	
Q360 □ 1961	40,064	3	4
Q361 □ 1961D	83,657	3	
Q362 □ 1962	39,374	3	4
Q363 □ 1962D	127,555	3	
Q364 □ 1963	77,392	3	4
Q365 □ 1963D	135,299	3	
Q366 □ 1964	564,341	3	4
Q367 □ 1964D	704,136	3	
Q368 □ 1965* COPPER-NICKEL CLAD	1,819,718	.75	
Q369 □ 1966	821,101	.75	
Q370 □ 1967	1,524,032	.75	
Q371 □ 1968	22,731	.75	
Q372 □ 1968D	101,534	.75	
Q373 □ 1968S PROOF ONLY	3,041		1
Q374 □ 1969	176,991	.75	
Q375 □ 1969D	114,368	.75	
Q376 □ 1969S PROOF ONLY	2,934		1

*QUARTERS MINTED 1965 AND LATER DID NOT CONTAIN SILVER
For worn silver see note at bottom of page 82.

DATE	Mintages in 1000's	Unc.	Proof
Q377 ☐ 1970	136,420	.75	
Q378 ☐ 1970D	417,342	.75	
Q379 ☐ 1970S Proof Only	2,633		1
Q380 ☐ 1971	109,284	.75	
Q381 ☐ 1971D	258,635	.75	
Q382 ☐ 1971S Proof Only	3,221		1
Q383 ☐ 1972	215,048	.75	
Q384 ☐ 1972D	311,068	.75	
Q385 ☐ 1972S Proof Only	3,261		1
Q386 ☐ 1973	346,924	.75	
Q387 ☐ 1973D	232,978	.75	
Q388 ☐ 1973S Proof Only	2,761		1
Q389 ☐ 1974	801,456	.75	
Q390 ☐ 1974D	353,161	.75	
Q391 ☐ 1974S Proof Only	2,613		1
Q392 ☐ 1976	809,784	.75	
Q393 ☐ 1976D	860,119	.75	
Q394 ☐ 1976S Proof Only	7,060		1
Q395 ☐ 1976S Silver Clad	15,000	2	3
Q396 ☐ 1977	468,556	.75	
Q397 ☐ 1977D	256,525	.75	
Q398 ☐ 1977S Proof Only	3,252		1
Q399 ☐ 1978	521,452	.75	
Q400 ☐ 1978D	287,374	.75	
Q401 ☐ 1978S Proof Only	3,128		1

Q402 □ 1979	515,708	.75	
Q403 □ 1979D	489,790	.75	
Q404 □ 1979S	3,678		1
Q405 □ 1979S * Proof Only			4
Q406 □ 1980P	635,832	.75	
Q407 □ 1980D	518,328	.75	
Q408 □ 1980S Proof Only	3,555		1
Q409 □ 1981P	601,716	.75	
Q410 □ 1981D	575,723	.75	
Q411 □ 1981S Proof Only	4,064		1
Q412 □ 1981S ** Proof Only			3
Q413 □ 1982P		.75	
Q414 □ 1982D		.75	
Q415 □ 1982S Proof Only			1

*Type 2 Clear S. **Type 2 New Clearer S.

HALF DOLLARS - 1794 TO DATE
Similiar in design to the other denominations of the same years, this series abounds in over dates and legend variations, making it attractive to numismatists.

FLOWING HAIR 1794-1795

	DATE	Mintages in 1000's	A.D.P. (F)	Good	V.Good	Fine	V.Fine	Ex.Fine
F1	☐1794	23	1,000	1,100	1,550	2,150	3,350	4,500
F2	☐1795	300	350	420	480	690	1,075	2,125
F3	☐1795 Recut dt		350	420	480	690	1,075	2,125
F4	☐1795 Three leaves under each wing			550	650	950	1,100	2,200	3,500

DRAPED BUST, SMALL EAGLE 1796-1797

DATE	Mintages in 1000's	A.D.P. (F)	Good	V.Good	Fine	V.Fine	Ex.Fine
F6 ☐ 1796 (15 stars)	Part of	8,000	9,000	11,500	15,125	22,000	29,000
F7 ☐ 1796 (16 stars)	1797 amt	8,000	9,000	11,500	15,125	22,000	29,000
F8 ☐ 1797...................	4	8,000	9,000	11,500	15,125	22,000	29,000

DRAPED BUST, EAGLE ON REVERSE, 1801-1807

DATE	Mintages in 1000's	A.D.P. (F)	V.Good	Fine	V.Fine	Ex.Fine	AU	Unc.
F9 ☐ 1801	30	375	325	650	975	1,450	3,000	9,000
F11 ☐ 1802	30	375	300	650	975	1,250	1,750	7,650
F12 ☐ 1803	188	110	125	200	550	1,000	1,450	6,500
F18 ☐ 1805	212	80	85	150	360	660	1,150	4,525
F16 ☐ 1805 Over 4 ...		160	150	285	595	875	1,250	4,525
F19 ☐ 1806		80	85	150	360	660	1,150	4,525
F20 ☐ 1806 Over 5 ...	840	80	90	155	400	700	1,200	4,525
F24 ☐ 1806/ inverted 6		130	140	250	500	800	1,300	5,000
F27 ☐ 1807	301	80	85	150	360	660	1,150	4,525

HALF DOLLARS - TURBAN HEAD OR CAPPED BUST 1807-1836

Motto Above Eagle, Lettered Edge, Lg. Size 1807-36

DATE	Mintages in 1000's	A.D.P. (F)	Fine	V.Fine	Ex.Fine	AU	Unc.
F28 ☐1807 sm. stars		60	150	350	700	1,250	1,750
F29 ☐1807 lg. stars	750	50	100	175	350	500	1,250
F30 ☐1807 50c/20c..........		35	70	125	250	350	1,200
F32 ☐1808.................	1,369	30	45	60	110	300	900
F31 ☐1808 Over 7		20	45	60	110	300	1,000
F33 ☐1809.................	1,406	20	45	60	110	300	900
F34 ☐1810.................	1,276	20	45	60	110	275	750
F35 ☐1811.................	1,204	20	45	60	110	275	750
F39 ☐1812.................	1,628	20	45	60	110	275	750
F40 ☐1812 Over 11		25	75	125	250	400	1,000
F42 ☐1813.................	1,242	20	45	60	110	205	700
F44 ☐1814.................	1,039	20	45	60	110	205	700
F45 ☐1814 Over 13		25	50	95	150	400	1,000
F47 ☐1815 Over 12	47	550	1,000	1,500	1,975	2,250	4,500
F50 ☐1817.................	1,216	20	45	60	110	205	700
F48 ☐1817 Over 13		75	150	300	450	650	1,500
F55 ☐1818.................	1,960	20	40	55	105	200	700
F54 ☐1818 Over 17		20	45	60	110	300	800
F58 ☐1819.................	2,208	20	40	55	105	200	700
F56 ☐1819/18		20	40	55	110	300	800

DATE	Mintages in 1000's	A.D.P. (F)	Fine	V.Fine	Ex.Fine	AU	Unc.
F59 ☐1820.................	751	18	35	50	100	195	700
F60 ☐1820 Over 19		18	50	75	150	295	800
F63 ☐1821.................	1,306	18	35	75	150	300	900
F65 ☐1822.................	1,560	18	35	50	100	195	690
F64 ☐1822 Over 21		40	75	125	250	300	800
F66 ☐1823.................	1,694	18	35	50	100	195	690
F76 ☐1824.................	3,505	18	35	50	100	195	690
F73 ☐1824 Over 21		18	35	50	100	210	750
F77 ☐1825.................	2,943	18	35	50	100	195	690
F79 ☐1826.................	4,044	18	35	50	100	195	690
F81 ☐1827 Squarebase 2 ...	5,493	18	35	50	100	195	690
F84 ☐1828.................	3,075	18	35	50	100	195	690
F89 ☐1829.................	3,712	18	35	50	100	195	690
F90 ☐1829 Over 27		18	35	50	100	195	700
F95 ☐1830.................	4,765	18	35	50	100	195	690
F99 ☐1831.................	5,874	18	35	50	100	195	690
F104 ☐1832.................	4,797	18	35	50	100	195	690
F106 ☐1833.................	5,206	18	35	50	100	195	690
F108 ☐1834.................	6,412	18	35	50	100	195	690
F114 ☐1835.................	5,352	18	35	50	100	195	690
F119 ☐1836	6,546	18	35	50	100	195	690
F120 ☐1836 Ltd. edge 50 over 00		40	75	200	350	550	1,250

HALF DOLLARS
TURBAN HEAD OR CAPPED BUST, NO MOTTO
ABOVE EAGLE, REEDED EDGE, REDUCED SIZE, 1836-1839

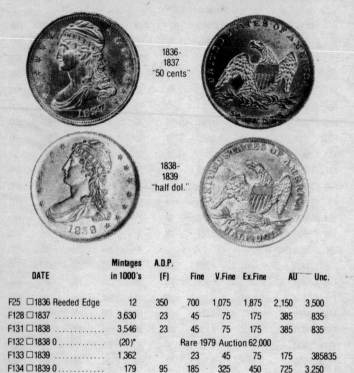

1836-
1837
"50 cents"

1838-
1839
"half dol."

DATE	Mintages in 1000's	A.D.P. (F)	Fine	V.Fine	Ex.Fine	AU	Unc.
F25 ☐1836 Reeded Edge	12	350	700	1,075	1,875	2,150	3,500
F128 ☐1837	3,630	23	45	75	175	385	835
F131 ☐1838	3,546	23	45	75	175	385	835
F132 ☐1838 0	(20)*	Rare 1979 Auction 62,000					
F133 ☐1839	1,362		23	45	75	175	385835
F134 ☐1839 0	179	95	185	325	450	725	3,250

*Total Mintage — no official mint record available

HALF DOLLARS
LIBERTY SEATED WITHOUT MOTTO ABOVE EAGLE, 1839-1866

These halves went through the same weight and design changes as the concurrent smaller denominations. The 1861-0 issue was minted mainly by the Confederate States, whose forces seized the mint on January 31, 1861, after some 330,000 coins had been struck. Something over 2,000,000 more were minted until the mint closed down on May 31st, 1861. Thus, although a Confederate coin was designed but never minted, the 1861-0 half was actually the only circulating silver Confederate coin.

(Mint Mark is below Eagle on Reverse)

DATE	Mintages in 1000's	A.D.P. (F)	Fine	V.Fine	Ex.Fine	AU	Unc.
F136 ☐ 1839................	1,972	12	25	35	70	150	600
F138 ☐ 1840 sm. ltrs.	1,435	12	25	35	70	150	600
F137 ☐ 1840 lg. ltrs.		120	225	300	500	750	2,000
F139 ☐ 1840 0	885	12	25	35	70	150	600
F142 ☐ 1841.................	310	35	65	120	245	375	1,000
F143 ☐ 1841 0	401	15	30	55	110	275	1,000
F145 ☐ 1842 sm. dt.	21	21	40	65	125	150	850
F146 ☐ 1842 lg. dt............	1,822	11	20	30	52	120	525
F148 ☐ 1842 0	957	11	20	30	52	120	525
F149 ☐ 1843.................	3,844	11	20	30	52	120	525
F150 ☐ 1843 0	2,268	11	20	30	52	125	550
F151 ☐ 1844.................	1,766	11	20	30	52	120	525
F152 ☐ 1844 0	2,005	11	20	30	52	120	550
F155 ☐ 1845.................	589	30	85	140	250	350	750
F156 ☐ 1845 0	2,094	11	20	30	52	120	525
F160 ☐ 1846 sm. dt.	2,210	11	20	30	52	120	525
F161 ☐ 1846 tall dt...........		11	20	30	52	120	525

HALF DOLLARS
LIBERTY SEATED WITHOUT MOTTO
OVER EAGLE 1846-1856

DATE	Mintages in 1000's	A.D.P. (F)	Fine	V.Fine	Ex.Fine	AU	Unc.
F162 ☐1846 Over 6		65	125	200	350	500	1,500
F164 ☐1846 0 Sm. dt.	2,304	11	20	30	52	120	525
F167 ☐1846 0 Lg. dt.		45	85	150	250	500	2,000
F168 ☐1847	1,156	11	20	30	52	120	525
F170 ☐1847 0	2,584	11	20	30	52	120	525
F171 ☐1848	580	30	40	60	75	150	525
F172 ☐1848 0	3,180	11	20	30	52	120	525
F173 ☐1849	1,252	11	20	30	52	120	525
F176 ☐1849 0	2,310	11	20	30	52	120	525
F177 ☐1850	227	65	120	185	325	550	1,500
F178 ☐1850 0	2,456	11	20	30	52	120	525
F179 ☐1851	201	55	100	210	350	550	1,800
F180 ☐1851 0	402	11	20	30	52	120	525
F181 ☐1852	77	105	200	300	500	750	1,900
F182 ☐1852 0	144	65	125	185	350	500	1,500
F184 ☐1853 arrows, rays	3,533	16	30	77	205	400	1,800
F185 ☐1853 0 arrows, rays . .	1,328	16	30	77	205	400	1,800
F186 ☐1854 arrows	2,982	11	20	36	90	235	835
F187 ☐1854 0 arrows.	5,240	11	20	36	90	235	835
F190 ☐1855 arrows*	759	11	20	36	90	235	835
F192 ☐1855 0 arrows.	3,688	11	20	36	90	235	835
F194 ☐1855S arrows	130	220	425	850	2,150	2,500	RARE
F195 ☐1856*	938	11	20	30	52	120	525
F196 ☐1856 0	2,658	11	20	30	52	120	525

*Proofs: 1855, 4,000, 1856, $2,000

HALF DOLLARS
LIBERTY SEATED WITHOUT MOTTO
ABOVE EAGLE 1856-1866 (Cont'd.)

Date	Mintages in 1000's	A.D.P. (F)	Good	Fine	V.Fine	Ex.Fine	Unc.	Proof
F198 ☐ 1856S	211	25	45	135	275	500	1,500	
F199 ☐ 1857	1,988	11	20	30	52	120	525	1,800
F200 ☐ 1857 0	818	11	20	30	52	120	550	
F201 ☐ 1857S	158	18	60	160	350	500	1,400	
F203 ☐ 1858	4,226	11	20	30	52	120	525	1,600
F204 ☐ 1858 0	7,294	11	20	30	52	120	525	
F205 ☐ 1858S	476	13	25	35	57	125	550	
F208 ☐ 1859	748	11	20	30	52	120	525	550
F209 ☐ 1859 0	2,834	11	20	30	52	120	·525	
F210 ☐ 1859S	566	13	25	35	57	125	575	
F212 ☐ 1860	304	13	25	35	57	125	550	550
F213 ☐ 1860 0	1,290	11	20	30	52	120	550	
F214 ☐ 1860S	472	13	25	35	57	125	575	
F215 ☐ 1861	2,888	11	20	30	52	120	525	550
F216 ☐ 1861 0	2,532	11	20	30	52	120	525	
F218 ☐ 1861S	938	11	20	30	52	120	550	
F220 ☐ 1862	252	38	70	95	175	250	600	550
F221 ☐ 1862S	1,352	11	20	30	52	120	525	
F224 ☐ 1863	504	13	25	35	57	125	600	550
F225 ☐ 1863S	916	11	20	30	52	120	525	
F226 ☐ 1864	380	16	30	40	62	130	600	550
F227 ☐ 1864S	658	11	20	30	52	120	525	
F230 ☐ 1865	512	13	25	35	57	125	600	550
F231 ☐ 1865S	675	11	20	30	52	120	525	
F232 ☐ 1866	UNIQUE							
F233 ☐ 1866S	60	80	150	215	425	750	4,950	

In 1873 the coin's weight was increased to 192.9 grains, accomplished by placing arrows at the date. These were again removed in 1875.

Arrows at Date   No Arrows at Date

Date	Mintages in 1000's(F)	A.D.P. Fine	V.Fine	Ex.Fine	AU	Unc.	Proof	
F234 ☐ 1866	746	9	17	26	45	115	495	510
F235 ☐ 1865S	1,054	9	17	26	45	115	495	
F236 ☐ 1867	449	12	23	90	150	225	725	510
F237 ☐ 1867S	1,196	9	17	26	45	115	495	
F238 ☐ 1868	418	9	17	26	45	115	495	510
F239 ☐ 1868S	1,160	9	17	26	45	115	495	
F240 ☐ 1869	796	9	17	26	45	115	495	510
F241 ☐ 1869S	656	9	17	26	45	115	775	
F242 ☐ 1870	635	9	17	30	50	125	550	510
F244 ☐ 1870CC	55	525	1,000	1,650	3,000	RARE	RARE	
F243 ☐ 1870S	1,004	9	17	26	45	115	495	
F245 ☐ 1871	1,205	9	17	26	45	115	495	510
F247 ☐ 1871CC	154	70	125	250	550	725	4,000	

HALF DOLLARS
LIBERTY SEATED WITH MOTTO OVER EAGLE 1871-1876

DATE	Mintages in 1000's	A.D.P. (F)	Fine	V.Fine	Ex.Fine	AU	Unc.	Proof
F246 ☐ 1871S.............	2,178	9	17	26	45	115	495	
F248 ☐ 1872.............	882	9	17	26	45	115	495	510
F250 ☐ 1872CC ..,......	257	50	95	150	340	650	1,600	
F249 ☐ 1872S.............	580	10	20	36	75	150	900	
F252 ☐ 1873 no arrows....	801	9	17	26	45	115	495	510
F253 ☐ 1873CC no arrows .	122	55	110	240	440	650	2,350	
F254 ☐ 1873 w/arrows....	1,816	16	30	77	210	385	900	990
F258 ☐ 1873CC w/arrows .	215	36	70	180	385	575	1,650	
F257 ☐ 1873S w/arrows...	228	21	40	110	285	375	1,250	
F259 ☐ 1874 w/arrows....	2,360	16	30	77	210	385	900	990
F261 ☐ 1874CC w/arrows .	59	180	350	500	925	1,250	4,500	
F260 ☐ 1874S w/arrows...	394	18	35	85	170	500	1,800	
NO ARROWS AT DATE								
F262 ☐ 1875.............	6,027	9	17	26	45	115	495	510
F265 ☐ 1875CC	1,008	9	17	26	45	115	495	
F263 ☐ 1875S.............	3,200	9	17	26	45	115	495	
F267 ☐ 1876.............	8,419	9	17	26	45	115	495	510
F270 ☐ 1876CC	1,956	9	17	26	45	115	495	
F269 ☐ 1876S.............	4,528	9	17	26	45	115	495	

HALF DOLLARS
LIBERTY SEATED W/ MOTTO ABOVE EAGLE, 1877-1891 (Cont'd.)

DATE	Mintages in 1000's	A.D.P. (F)	Fine	V.Fine	Ex.Fine	AU	Unc.	Proof
F271 ☐ 1877	8,305	9	17	26	45	115	495	510
F273 ☐ 1877CC	1,420	9	17	26	45	115	495	
F272 ☐ 1877S	5,365	9	17	26	45	115	495	
F274 ☐ 1878	1,378	9	17	26	45	115	495	510
F276 ☐ 1878CC	62	160	300	525	1,050	1,500	2,200	
F275 ☐ 1878S	12	1,600	3,200	4,400	6,100	7,500	20,000	
F277 ☐ 1879	6	170	325	400	525	650	1,000	510
F278 ☐ 1880	10	140	275	330	450	550	975	510
F279 ☐ 1881	11	140	265	330	425	550	975	510
F280 ☐ 1882	5	170	325	400	500	600	1,025	510
F281 ☐ 1883	9	150	275	315	450	550	950	510
F282 ☐ 1884	5	180	340	400	500	600	1,025	510
F283 ☐ 1885	6	180	340	390	480	575	1,025	510
F284 ☐ 1886	6	180	350	435	500	600	1,025	510
F285 ☐ 1887	6	180	350	435	500	600	1,025	510
F286 ☐ 1888	13	130	250	310	400	500	950	510
F287 ☐ 1889	13	130	250	310	400	500	950	510
F288 ☐ 1890	13	130	250	310	400	500	950	510
F289 ☐ 1891	201	26	50	80	190	275	825	510

HALF DOLLARS - LIBERTY HEAD OR BARBER, 1892-1915

The familiar Barber design appears once again. As with his dimes and quarters, Barber's initial "B" is found at the base of the bust neck on the obverse.

(Mint Mark is Below Eagle on Reverse)

DATE	Mintages in 1000's	A.D.P. (F)	Fine	V.Fine	Ex.Fine	AU	Unc.	Proof
F290 ☐ 1892*	935	12	26	42	143	275	550	540
F291 ☐ 1892 O	390	75	145	230	350	510	900	
F294 ☐ 1892S	1,029	75	145	230	330	480	925	
F295 ☐ 1893*	1,827	12	26	42	143	275	550	540
F296 ☐ 1893 O	1,389	20	36	82	235	340	690	
F297 ☐ 1893S	740	45	81	180	303	440	900	
F298 ☐ 1894*	1,149	12	24	54	143	275	550	540
F299 ☐ 1894 O	2,138	12	26	58	200	315	625	
F300 ☐ 1894S	4,049	12	24	55	187	300	585	
F301 ☐ 1895*	1,735	10	23	47	132	275	565	540
F302 ☐ 1895 O	1,766	12	24	50	175	330	645	
F303 ☐ 1895S	1,108	15	32	70	187	330	590	
F304 ☐ 1896	951	13	27	48	150	290	565	540
F305 ☐ 1896 O	924	20	39	90	260	395	900	
F306 ☐ 1896S	1,141	35	77	175	320	465	990	
F307 ☐ 1897	2,481	9	19	35	125	330	530	540
F308 ☐ 1897 O	632	36	72	185	360	635	1,265	

See note at bottom of page 82.

HALF DOLLARS - LIBERTY HEAD OR BARBER 1897-1906

DATE	Mintages in 1000's	A.D.P. (F)	Fine	V.Fine	Ex.Fine	AU	Unc.	Proof
F309 ☐ 1897S	934	60	120	195	330	515	1,075	
F310 ☐ 1898	2,957	8	17	33	120	230	530	540
F311 ☐ 1898 O	874	14	29	75	230	330	635	
F312 ☐ 1898S	2,359	10	23	46	175	320	590	
F313 ☐ 1899	5,539	8	17	33	120	230	530	540
F314 ☐ 1899 O	1,724	12	24	51	205	320	635	
F315 ☐ 1899S	1,686	10	23	46	175	300	590	
F316 ☐ 1900	4,763	8	17	33	120	230	530	540
F317 ☐ 1900 O	2,744	10	23	46	220	330	660	
F318 ☐ 1900S	2,560	10	22	42	175	240	590	
F319 ☐ 1901	4,269	8	17	33	120	230	530	540
F320 ☐ 1901 O	1,124	13	27	55	255	420	1,020	
F321 ☐ 1901S	847	18	36	120	360	635	1,130	
F322 ☐ 1902	4,923	8	17	33	120	230	530	540
F323 ☐ 1902 O	2,526	10	22	39	170	320	660	
F324 ☐ 1902S	1,461	10	22	47	180	330	625	
F325 ☐ 1903	2,279	8	17	33	120	230	530	540
F326 ☐ 1903 O	2,100	10	22	39	165	315	625	
F327 ☐ 1903S	1,921	10	22	42	175	330	625	
F328 ☐ 1904	2,993	8	17	33	120	230	530	540
F329 ☐ 1904 O	1,118	13	27	60	255	440	990	
F330 ☐ 1904S	553	19	38	108	315	530	925	
F331 ☐ 1905	663	13	28	69	205	350	625	540
F332 ☐ 1905 O	505	16	32	77	235	385	660	
F333 ☐ 1905S	2,494	10	22	39	125	315	625	
F334 ☐ 1906	2,639	8	17	33	120	230	530	540
F335 ☐ 1906D	4,028	10	22	36	140	260	550	
F336 ☐ 1906 O	2,446	10	22	37	150	275	570	

See note at bottom of page 82.

HALF DOLLARS - LIBERTY HEAD OR BARBER, 1906-1915

DATE	Mintages in 1000's	A.D.P. (VF)	V.Fine	Ex.Fine	AU	Unc.	Proof
F337 ☐ 1906S	1,740	20	41	165	295	590	
F338 ☐ 1907	2,599	15	33	120	230	530	540
F339 ☐ 1907 D	3,856	16	35	140	260	550	
F340 ☐ 1907 0	3,947	16	35	140	265	570	
F341 ☐ 1907 S	1,250	22	46	185	290	625	
F342 ☐ 1908	1,355	15	33	120	230	530	540
F343 ☐ 1908D	3,280	16	35	130	240	550	
F344 ☐ 1908 0	5,360	16	35	140	250	550	
F345 ☐ 1908S	1,645	20	44	175	300	590	
F346 ☐ 1909	2,369	15	33	120	230	530	540
F347 ☐ 1909 0	925	30	60	230	440	690	
F348 ☐ 1909S	1,764	19	39	165	295	590	
F349 ☐ 1910	419	29	58	220	385	645	540
F350 ☐ 1910S	1,948	19	39	165	290	585	
F351 ☐ 1911	1,407	15	33	120	230	530	540
F352 ☐ 1911D	696	19	40	150	265	575	
F353 ☐ 1911S	1,272	17	36	150	280	585	
F354 ☐ 1912	1,551	15	33	120	230	530	540
F355 ☐ 1912D	2,301	16	35	140	230	530	
F356 ☐ 1912S	1,370	17	36	150	280	585	
F357 ☐ 1913	189	42	85	215	385	770	540
F358 ☐ 1913D	534	23	47	150	265	530	
F359 ☐ 1913S	604	32	65	175	345	625	
F360 ☐ 1914	125	60	130	285	495	695	875
F361 ☐ 1914S	992	25	50	165	320	585	
F362 ☐ 1915	138	45	90	230	420	815	875
F363 ☐ 1915D	1,170	15	33	120	230	530	
F364 ☐ 1915S	1,604	17	36	135	260	570	

See note at bottom of page 82.

HALF DOLLARS - LIBERTY WALKING, 1916-1920

A truly magnificent coin that was perhaps inspired by the earlier work of St. Gaudens, "LIBERTY" carries olive branches of peace as she beckons toward the dawn of a new day. The design reflects the sentiment of a nation at war yet yearning for peace. Designed by A.A. Weinman, whose initials "AW" appear under the tip of the eagle's wing feathers at the lower right in a very artistic monogram. It must be magnified to be fully appreciated. No proofs were minted until 1936.

(Mint Mark is Under "In God We Trust" on 1916 and Early 1917. Later Left of "H" on Reverse.

DATE	Mintages in 1000's	A.D.P. (VF)	V.Fine	Ex.Fine	AU	UNC.
F365 ☐ 1916	608	55	105	180	290	385
F366 ☐ 1916D on obverse	1,014	30	55	120	195	330
F367 ☐ 1916S on obverse	508	110	210	330	465	715
F368 ☐ 1917	12,292	9	17	30	55	140
F369 ☐ 1917D on obverse	765	38	72	150	240	465
F370 ☐ 1917D on reverse	1,940	23	42	115	230	495
F371 ☐ 1917S on obverse	952	75	140	330	480	900
F372 ☐ 1917S on reverse	5,554	12	22	40	85	240
F373 ☐ 1918	6,634	21	39	110	220	330
F374 ☐ 1918D	3,853	23	44	120	255	660
F375 ☐ 1918S	10,282	12	25	45	90	240
F376 ☐ 1919	962	55	105	320	515	960
F377 ☐ 1919D	1,165	60	120	385	750	1,925
F378 ☐ 1919S	1,552	45	85	345	690	1,740
F379 ☐ 1920	6,372	10	20	50	95	240

HALF DOLLARS - LIBERTY WALKING 1920-1939 (con't)

DATE	Mintages in 1000's	A.D.P. (VF)	V.Fine	Ex.Fine	AU	Unc.	Proof
F380 ☐ 1920D	1,551	50	95	230	485	960	
F381 ☐ 1920S	4,624	17	32	100	330	770	
F382 ☐ 1921	246	200	385	900	1,350	2,000	
F383 ☐ 1921D	208	240	460	990	1,450	2,150	
F384 ☐ 1921S	548	95	180	990	2,550	6,000	
F385 ☐ 1923S	2,178	20	37	130	330	840	
F386 ☐ 1927S	2,392	11	22	75	220	690	
F387 ☐ 1928S	1,940	13	26	88	250	770	
F388 ☐ 1929D	1,001	10	18	60	130	330	
F389 ☐ 1929S	1,902	7	14	55	120	330	
F390 ☐ 1933S	1,786	5	10	33	100	305	
F391 ☐ 1934	6,964			13	27	81	
F392 ☐ 1934D	2,361			27	55	162	
F393 ☐ 1934S	3,652			20	55	305	
F394 ☐ 1935	9,162			11	21	60	
F395 ☐ 1935D	3,004			27	55	170	
F396 ☐ 1935S	3,854			22	66	205	
F397 ☐ 1936	12,618			11	20	55	750
F398 ☐ 1936D	4,252			20	42	110	
F399 ☐ 1936S	3,884			20	39	132	
F400 ☐ 1937	9,528			11	22	58	500
F401 ☐ 1937D	1,760			30	72	209	
F402 ☐ 1937S	2,090			20	48	150	
F403 ☐ 1938	4,118			14	29	96	375
F404 ☐ 1938D	492			85	220	360	
F405 ☐ 1939	6,821			12	22	81	325

See note at bottom of page 82.

DATE	Mintages in 1000's	A.D.P. (F)	Good	Fine	V.Fine	E.Fine
F406 ☐ 1939D	4,268		14	22	72	
F407 ☐ 1939S	2,552		16	33	108	
F408 ☐ **1940**	9,167		10	14	44	295
F409 ☐ 1940S	4,550		14	22	91	
F410 ☐ 1941	24,207			11	33	295
F411 ☐ 1941D	11,248			16	51	
F412 ☐ 1941S	8,098			44	138	
F413 ☐ 1942	47,839			11	33	295
F414 ☐ 1942D	10,974			16	60	
F415 ☐ 1942S	12,708			33	77	
F416 ☐ 1943	53,190			11	33	
F417 ☐ 1943D	11,346			17	66	
F418 ☐ 1943S	13,450			24	84	
F419 ☐ 1944	28,206			11	33	
F420 ☐ 1944D	9,769			16	50	
F421 ☐ 1944S	8,904			20	72	
F422 ☐ 1945	31,502			11	33	
F423 ☐ 1945D	9,966			15	50	
F424 ☐ 1945S	10,156			18	69	
F425 ☐ 1946	12,118			12	36	
F426 ☐ 1946D	2,151			24	48	
F427 ☐ 1946S	3,724			20	69	
F428 ☐ 1947	4,094			26	72	
F429 ☐ 1947D	3,900			18	60	

See note at bottom of page 82.

HALF DOLLARS - FRANKLIN OR LIBERTY BELL, 1948-1952

Benjamin Franklin has the distinction, among many others, of being honored on a coin even though he was not a president of the U.S. The Liberty Bell is an appropriate symbol for the reverse, especially since Franklin did not feel the eagle should be used on a coin. The designer included the eagle on the reverse, but of diminished size. On the bell is shown the mark of the firm that repaired the crack, Pass & Stow of Philadelphia

Mint Mark is Above Liberty Bell on Reverse

DATE	Mintages in 1000's	A.D.P. (EF)	Ex.Fine	AU	Unc.	Proof
F430 ☐ 1948	3,007			9	15	
F431 ☐ 1948D	4,029			9	14	
F432 ☐ 1949	5,614			15	75	
F433 ☐ 1949D	4,121			19	60	
F434 ☐ 1949S	3,744			75	150	
F435 ☐ 1950	7,794			9	50	225
F436 ☐ 1950D	8,032			9	30	
F437 ☐ 1951	16,860			9	15	130
F438 ☐ 1951D	9,475			10	50	
F439 ☐ 1951S	13,696			12	35	
F440 ☐ 1952	21,274			7	12	80
F441 ☐ 1952D	25,395			7	12	
F442 ☐ 1952S	5,526			15	30	

See note at bottom of page 82.

HALF DOLLARS
FRANKLIN OR LIBERTY BELL, 1953-1963

DATE	Mintages in 1000's	A.D.P. (EF)	Ex.Fine	AU	Unc.	Proof
F443 □ 1953	2,797			15	30	50
F444 □ 1953D	20,900			7	10	
F445 □ 1953S	4,148			9	15	
F446 □ 1954	13,422			7	10	30
F447 □ 1954D	25,446			7	10	
F448 □ 1954S	4,993			7	12	
F449 □ 1955	2,876			9	13	27
F450 □ 1956	4,701			9	14	14
F451 □ 1957	6,362			7	11	10
F452 □ 1957D	19,997			7	10	
F453 □ 1958	4,918				9	11
F454 □ 1958D	23,962				9	
F455 □ 1959	7,349				8	10
F456 □ 1959D	13,054				8	
F457 □ 1960	7,716				8	10
F458 □ 1960D	18,216				8	
F459 □ 1961	11,318				7	10
F460 □ 1961D	20,276				7	
F461 □ 1962	12,932				7	10
F462 □ 1962D	35,473				7	
F463 □ 1963	25,240				7	10
F464 □ 1963D	67,069				7	

See note at bottom of page 82.

Gilroy Roberts designed the obverse of this coin, after the assassination of President John F. Kennedy; Frank Gasparro designed the seal on the reverse. Although the Franklin design had been in circulation only a relatively short time, popular sentiment and demand gave birth to the new half.

Mint Mark 1964-1967   Mint Mark 1968

DATE	Mintages in 1000's	Unc.	Proof
F465 ☐ 1964	93,128	7	10
F466 ☐ 1964D	101,494	7	
F467 ☐ 1965 SILVER CLAD	155,780	3	
F468 ☐ 1966	108,985	3	
F469 ☐ 1967	295,046	3	
F470 ☐ 1968D	246,952	3	
F471 ☐ 1968S Proof only	3,042		4
F472 ☐ 1969D	130,212	3	
F473 ☐ 1969S Proof only	3,000		4

Mintage of silver half dollars (90%) ceased in 1965. From 1965-1970 they were minted in 40% silver, from 1971 on in copper-nickel.

HALF DOLLARS - JOHN F. KENNEDY - 1964 TO DATE (Cont'd.)
BICENTENNIAL DESIGN

DATE	Mintages in 1000's	Unc.	Proof
F474 ☐ 1970D ISSUED ONLY IN MINT SETS	2,150	30	
D475 ☐ 1970S Proof only	2,633		10
D476 ☐ 1971 COPPER NICKEL CLAD	155,164	1	
F477 ☐ 1971D	302,098	1	
F478 ☐ 1971S Proof only	3,224		2
F479 ☐ 1972	153,180	1	
F480 ☐ 1972D	141,890		
F481 ☐ 1972S Proof only	3,268		2
F482 ☐ 1973	64,964	1	
F483 ☐ 1973D	83,171	1	
F484 ☐ 1973S Proof only	2,769		2
F485 ☐ 1974	201,596	1	
F486 ☐ 1974D	79,066	1	
F487 ☐ 1974S Proof only	2,617		3
F488 ☐ 1976	71,240	1	
F489 ☐ 1976D	72,119	1	
F490 ☐ 1976S (clad) Proof only	4,150		2
F491 ☐ 1976S (.400 silver)	15,000	3	4
F492 ☐ 1977	43,598	1	
F493 ☐ 1977D	31,449	1	
F494 ☐ 1977S Proof only	3,251		2
F495 ☐ 1978	14,350	1	
F496 ☐ 1978D	13,765	1	
F497 ☐ 1978S Proof only	3,127		3
F498 ☐ 1979	68,312	1	
F499 ☐ 1979D	15,816	1	
F500 ☐ 1979S Proof only Filled S	3,677		3
F501 ☐ 1979S Proof only Clear S			25
F502 ☐ 1980P	44,134	1	

F503 ☐1980D	33,457	1	
F504 ☐1980S Proof only	3,555		2
F505 ☐1981P	29,544	.1	
F506 ☐1981D	27,840	1	
F507 ☐1981S Proof only	4,063	1	2
F508 ☐1981S** Proof only			25

SILVER DOLLARS - 1794-1935

Early coins weigh 416 grains, of 89.24% silver and 10.76% copper. Denomination is on the edge of the coin. Measuring 1½ inches in diameter, the silver dollar is the largest U.S. coin. Weight was reduced in 1804 to 412½ grains, and silver content went up to 90%

LIBERTY WITH FLOWING HAIR, 1794-1795

DATE	Mintages in 1000's	A.D.P. (F)	Good	Fine	V.Fine	Ex.Fine	AU	Unc.
S1 ☐1794	(1,758)*	8,000	6,350	13,000	21,500	42,000	60,000	RARE
S2 ☐1795	160	800	925	1,700	2,400	4,500	8,800	40,000

*Total mintage

DRAPED BUST SMALL EAGLE ON REVERSE, 1795-1798

DATE	Mintages in 1000's	A.D.P. (F)	Good	Fine	V.Fine	Ex.Fine	AU	Unc.
S3 ☐1795	43	800	850	1,700	2,150	3,850	5,900	13,750
S6 ☐1796	73	700	850	1,375	1,959	2,800	4,800	11,550
S10 ☐1797 Sm. Ltrs.	(7,776)*	1,350	1,200	2,700	3,750	5,500	6,950	20,000
S9 ☐1797 Lg. Ltrs.		700	815	1,325	1,950	2,800	4,800	11,550
S11 ☐1798 13 Stars	328	1,200	875	2,500	3,500	4,100	5,900	16,500
S12 ☐1798 15 Stars		1,500	1,200	2,900	3,750	4,850	6,150	16,500

*Total Mintage

DRAPED BUST, HERALDIC EAGLE REVERSE, 1798-1804

DATE	Mintages in 1000's	A.D.P. (G)	Good	Fine	V.Fine	Ex.Fine	AU	Unc.
S13 ☐1798 all var.		200	320	510	690	1,175	2,175	6,650
S14 ☐1799 all var.	424	200	320	510	690	1,175	2,175	6,650
S19 ☐1800 all var.	221	200	325	510	690	1,175	2,175	6,650
S20 ☐1801	54	200	350	600	925	1,550	2,400	6,650
S22 ☐1802	42	200	340	570	825	1,300	2,250	6,650
S21 ☐1802 over 1 ...		200	325	515	700	1,180	2,190	6,650
S24 ☐1803	66	200	325	515	700	1,180	2,190	6,650

☐1804 One of the most valuable coins in the world — about 15 known.
Last one sold for $190,000 (EF in 1982)

SILVER DOLLARS
LIBERTY SEATED (GOBRECHT) 1836-1839

These were actually patterns and never released, although a few of the 1836 issue did find their way into circulation. All are rare. All struck in proof only.

DATE	Mintages in 1000's	A.D.P. (VF)	V.Fine	Ex.Fine	AU	Proof
☐ 1836	(1,025)*	1,000	1,500	2,050	2,300	6,000
☐ 1838	(31)*	1,100	1,750	2,250	2,900	11,500
☐ 1839	(303)*	1,500	2,000	2,500	3,700	13,500

*Total Mintage

LIBERTY SEATED, MO MOTTO OVER EAGLE, 1840-1873

Mint Mark
is Below Eagle
on Reverse

DATE	Mintages in 1000's	A.D.P. (VF)	V.Fine	Ex.Fine	AU	Unc.	Proof
S25 □ 1840	61	100	200	275	450	750	5,000
S26 □ 1841	173	100	195	265	440	750	4,000
S27 □ 1842	185	100	195	265	440	750	4,000
S28 □ 1843	165	100	195	265	440	750	4,000
S29 □ 1844	20	200	400	550	850	1,500	1,250
S31 □ 1845	24	190	375	525	850	1,600	1,250
S32 □ 1846	111	100	195	265	440	925	1,250
S33 □ 1846 0	59	190	365	545	850	2,100	
S34 □ 1847	141	100	195	265	440	950	1,250
S35 □ 1848	15	250	550	700	950	1,750	1,250
S36 □ 1849	63	175	350	500	750	1,250	1,250
S37 □ 1850	7	350	700	1,050	1,250	3,000	1,250
S38 □ 1850 0	40	350	700	1,000	1,250	3,100	
S39 □ 1851 original*	1						
S40 □ 1852 original*	1						
S41 □ 1853	46	175	325	475	525	850	1,400
S42 □ 1854	33	450	975	1,450	1,850	2,950	4,000
S43 □ 1855	26	450	925	1,300	1,750	2,900	4,000
S44 □ 1856	63	175	365	625	850	1,600	3,000
S45 □ 1857	94	175	350	650	850	1,500	3,000
S46 □ 1858	(80)			PROOF ONLY			5,000
S47 □ 1859	256	300	575	695	850	1,600	975
S48 □ 1859 0	360	100	195	265	440	750	
S49 □ 1859S	20	350	525	825	1,150	3,100	
S50 □ 1860	219	250	525	675	950	1,700	975
S51 □ 1860 0	515	100	195	265	440	950	
S52 □ 1861	78	300	625	850	1,100	2,100	975
S53 □ 1862	12	300	600	825	1,050	2,050	975
S54 □ 1863	28	175	340	440	825	1,700	975
S55 □ 1864	31	175	325	415	750	1,600	975
S56 □ 1865	47	100	195	265	440	1,500	975

*Restrike in proof only — approximate price $5,000.

SILVER DOLLARS - LIBERTY SEATED
WITH "IN GOD WE TRUST" ADDED, 1866-1873

DATE	Mintages in 1000's	A.D.P. (VF)	V.Fine	Ex.Fine	AU	Unc.	Proof
S57 ☐ 1866	50	150	280	375	500	1,450	975
S58 ☐ 1867	47	140	275	365	500	1,450	975
S59 ☐ 1868	163	125	250	340	475	1,400	975
S60 ☐ 1869	424	100	195	265	440	775	975
S61 ☐ 1870	416	100	195	265	440	775	975
S63 ☐ 1870CC	12	250	540	650	850	2,200	
S62 ☐ 1870S	RARE		39,000	62,000			
S64 ☐ 1871	1,075	100	195	265	440	775	975
S65 ☐ 1871CC	1	1,100	2,150	3,000	4,250	7,500	
S66 ☐ 1872	1,106	100	195	265	440	775	975
S68 ☐ 1872CC	3	900	1,700	2,100	2,750	4,150	
S67 ☐ 1872S	9	300	585	850	1,250	2,500	
S69 ☐ 1873	294	140	265	375	500	1,325	975
S70 ☐ 1873CC	2	1,500	3,000	3,850	4,500	9,000	
☐ 1873S	(700)*	— No pieces are known to exist					

*Total Mintage.

SILVER DOLLARS - LIBERTY HEAD OR MORGAN
1878-1879

Many Morgan dollars, named for their designer George T. Morgan, exist in a proof-like (P/L) state. These are early strikes from the proof dies, and are highly collectable. True proof dollars have square edges, proof-likes are beveled, as proofs are struck twice by hand and P/Ls are struck once by machine. Prices for these start at double the uncirculated price, some common dollars being very scarce in P/L.

Mint Mart is below eagle on Reverse

DATE	Mintages in 1000's	A.D.P. (EF)	E.Fine	AU	Unc.	Proof
S73 ☐ 1878 7-tail feathers........	9,748	12	20	24	54	750
S71 ☐ 1878 8-tail feathers........	750	13	26	33	64	750
S72 ☐ 1878 7 over 8 feathers		15	32	42	72	
S75 ☐ 1878CC	2,212	17	40	55	126	
S74 ☐ 1878S	9,774	12	20	24	59	
S76 ☐ 1879......................	14,807	12	20	22	45	715
S80 ☐ 1879CC	756	90	205	330	465	
S77 ☐ 1879 0	2,887	12	20	24	60	
S78 ☐ 1879S	9,110	12	20	24	58	

Except for rare dates, silver dollars are not considered collectable in less than extra fine grade. Lower grade dollars are generally worth about ⅗ the daily spot price per ounce for silver.

Mintages A.D.P.

	DATE in 1000's	(EF)	E.Fine	AU	Unc.	Proof	
S81 ☐1880	12,601	12	20	22	45		715
S87 ☐1880CC	591	35	90	138	215		
S88 ☐1880CC over 79		35	84	120	205		
S83 ☐1880 O	5,305	12	20	26	78		
S86 ☐1880S	8,900	12	20	24	58		
S91 ☐1881	9,164	12	20	22	45		715
S94 ☐1881CC	296	45	102	132	205		
S92 ☐1881 O	5,708	12	18	22	48		
S93 ☐1881S	12,760	12	20	23	58		
S95 ☐1882	11,101	12	20	22	45		715
S99 ☐1882CC	1,133	20	40	53	92		
S96 ☐1882 O	6,090	12	18	22	50		
S97 ☐1882 O over S		12	20	25	60		
S98 ☐1882S	9,250	12	21	24	58		
S100 ☐1883	12,191	12	20	22	45		715
S103 ☐1883CC	1,204	20	40	53	92		
S101 ☐1883 O	8,725	12	18	22	45		
S102 ☐1883S	6,250	19	29	132	440		
S104 ☐1884	14,071	12	20	24	55		715
S108 ☐1884CC	1,136	20	40	53	92		
S106 ☐1884 O	9,730	12	18	22	45		
S107 ☐1884S	3,200	20	35	200	1,325		
S109 ☐1885	17,788	12	18	22	45		715
S112 ☐1885CC	228	75	163	168	209		
S110 ☐1885 O	9,185	12	18	22	45		
S111 ☐1885S	1,497	12	24	51	116		
S113 ☐1886	19,964	12	18	22	45		715
S114 ☐1886 O	10,710	12	22	48	347		
S115 ☐1886S	750	19	33	48	114		
S116 ☐1887	20,291	12	18	22	45		715
S118 ☐1887 O	11,550	12	20	26	55		
S120 ☐1887S	1,771	12	22	27	72		

SILVER DOLLARS - MORGAN DOLLAR 1888-1896

DATE	Mintages in 1000's	A.D.P. (EF)	Ex.Fine	AU	Unc.	Proof
S121 ☐ 1888	19,184	12	18	22	45	715
S122 ☐ 1888 0	12,150	12	20	23	45	
S123 ☐ 1888S	657	19	38	57	120	
S124 ☐ 1889	21,727	12	18	22	45	715
S127 ☐ 1889CC	350	300	644	1,675	4,500	
S125 ☐ 1889 0	11,875	12	21	26	90	
S126 ☐ 1889S	700	20	40	54	72	
S128 ☐ 1890	16,803	12	18	23	50	715
S131 ☐ 1890CC	2,309	20	41	66	228	
S129 ☐ 1890 0	10,701	12	20	24	60	
S130 ☐ 1890S	8,230	12	22	26	57	
S132 ☐ 1891	8,694	12	22	39	84	715
S136 ☐ 1891CC	1,618	20	41	66	193	
S133 ☐ 1891 0	7,955	12	22	36	77	
S135 ☐ 1891S	5,296	12	22	26	54	
S137 ☐ 1892	1,037	12	34	42	143	715
S140 ☐ 1892CC	1,352	40	80	193	330	
S138 ☐ 1892 0	2,744	12	24	42	120	
S139 ☐ 1892S	1,200	75	150	770	4,100	
S141 ☐ 1893	389	45	90	185	315	715
S144 ☐ 1893CC	677	165	330	480	810	
S142 ☐ 1893 0	300	120	240	385	1,020	
S143 ☐ 1893S	100	1,700	3,400	9,150	18,150	
S145 ☐ 1894	111	200	450	660	930	850
S146 ☐ 1894 0	1,723	16	33	77	480	
S147 ☐ 1894S	1,260	42	84	170	340	
S148 ☐ 1895		PROOF ONLY (880)				14,000
S149 ☐ 1895 0	450	150	300	535	1,925	
S150 ☐ 1895S	400	190	375	590	835	
S151 ☐ 1896S	9,977	12	18	22	45	715
S152 ☐ 1896 0	4,900	12	24	84	770	
S154 ☐ 1896S	5,000	45	90	215	420	

DATE	Mintages in 1000's	A.D.P. (EF)	Ex.Fine	AU	Unc.	Proof
S155 ☐ 1897	2,823	12	18	22	49	715
S156 ☐ 1897 O	4,004	12	23	48	385	
S157 ☐ 1897S	5,825	12	22	26	60	
S158 ☐ 1898	5,885	12	18	22	45	715
S159 ☐ 1898 O	4,440	12	22	26	45	
S160 ☐ 1898S	4,102	12	24	51	138	
S161 ☐ 1899	331	29	58	72	102	715
S162 ☐ 1899 O	12,290	12	22	24	46	
S164 ☐ 1899S	2,562	13	26	55	150	
S165 ☐ 1900	8,831	12	18	22	46	715
S166 ☐ 1900 O	12,590	12	22	26	46	
S169 ☐ 1900S	3,540	12	24	43	127	
S170 ☐ 1901	6,963	26	52	240	900	1,000
S172 ☐ 1901 O	13,320	12	24	27	50	
S173 ☐ 1901S	2,284	16	33	60	270	
S174 ☐ 1902	7,995	12	22	30	60	715
S175 ☐ 1902 O	8,636	12	22	24	45	
S176 ☐ 1902S	1,530	45	90	143	220	
S177 ☐ 1903	4,653	12	20	28	55	715
S178 ☐ 1903 O	4,450	96	193	210	153	
S179 ☐ 1903S	1,241	75	152	525	1,485	
S181 ☐ 1904	2,789	12	22	39	115	715
S182 ☐ 1904 O	3,720	12	22	26	45	
S183 ☐ 1904S	2,304	50	102	358	836	
S184 ☐ 1921	44,690	12	18	20	30	
S185 ☐ 1921D	20,345	12	18	20	32	
S186 ☐ 1921S	21,695	12	18	20	39	

See note at bottom of page 116.

SILVER DOLLARS - PEACE DOLLAR, 1921-1926

These were designed by Anthony DeFrancisci and dedicated to lasting peace. The 1921 issue in high relief proved impractical, and was modified for subsequent issues. These were discontinued after the issuance of the silver certificate of 1934 which specified as backing "one dollar in silver" rather than "one silver dollar" as previous. No proofs were issued.

DATE	Mintages in 1000's	A.D.P. (EF)	Ex.Fine	AU	Unc.
S187 ☐ 1921	1,006	12	41	66	220
S189 ☐ 1922	51,737	12	18	20	30
S190 ☐ 1922D	15,063	12	18	20	33
S191 ☐ 1922S	17,475	12	18	20	35
S192 ☐ 1923	30,800	12	18	20	30
S193 ☐ 1923D	6,811	12	18	20	36
S194 ☐ 1923S	19,020	12	18	20	36
S195 ☐ 1924	11,811	12	18	20	35
S196 ☐ 1924S	1,728	12	32	39	163
S197 ☐ 1925	10,198	12	18	20	35
S198 ☐ 1925S	1,610	12	19	27	107
S199 ☐ 1926	1,939	12	19	24	48

*Deeply struck specimens command 50%-100% premium. See note at bottom of page 116.

SILVER DOLLARS - PEACE DOLLAR 1926-1935

DATE	Mintages in 1000's	A.D.P. (EF)	Ex.Fine	AU	Unc.
S200 ☐1926D	2,349	12	20	29	72
S201 ☐1926S	6,980	12	18	20	48
S202 ☐1927	848	12	24	39	120
S203 ☐1927D	1,269	12	26	84	235
S204 ☐1927S	866	12	24	48	162
S205 ☐1928	361	66	132	143	240
S206 ☐1928S	1,632	12	21	42	127
S207 ☐1934	954	12	26	46	99
S208 ☐1934D	1,569	12	22	42	120
S209 ☐1934S	1,011	75	152	440	1,195
S210 ☐1935	1,576	12	20	26	66
S211 ☐1935S	1,964	12	21	42	170

See note at bottom of page 116.

EISENHOWER DOLLAR 1971-1974, 1977-1978

EISENHOWER DOLLARS 1971-1978

Created and issued primarily to serve the needs of the Las Vegas gambling industry.

DATE	Mintages in 1000's	Unc.	Proof
S212 □ 1971*	47,799	2	
S213 □ 1971D*	68,586	2	
S214 □ 1971S**	6,668	7	9
S215 □ 1972*	75,890	2	
S216 □ 1972D*	92,548	2	
S217 □ 1972S**	2,193	12	15
S218 □ 1973*	2,000	10	
S219 □ 1973D*	2,000	10	
S221 □ 1973S**	1,883	12	85
S220 □ 1973S*	2,769		5
S222 □ 1974*	27,366	2	
S223 □ 1974D*	35,466	2	
S225 □ 1974S**	1,306	12	21
S224 □ 1974S*	2,617		3
S226 □ 1976 var. I*	3,500	3	
S227 □ 1976 var. II*	30,329	2	
S228 □ 1976D var. I*	21,148	2	
S229 □ 1976D var. II*	3,407	2	
S230 □ 1976S**	1,045	8	10
S231 □ 1976S*	4,150		5
S232 □ 1977*	12,596	2	
S233 □ 1977D*	32,983	2	
S234 □ 1977S*	3,251		3

S235 □ 1978*	25,702	2	
S236 □ 1978D*	23,013	2	
S237 □ 1978S*	3,128		6

A total of 439,899 coins from both mints was melted in 1974.　*Copper nickel clad.　**Silver Clad

Variety I: Design in low relief. Bold lettering on reverse.
Variety II: Sharp design. Delicate lettering on reverse.

SUSAN B. ANTHONY DOLLARS - 1979 TO 1981

Smaller dollar issued to replace large size Eisenhower Dollar. Proven very unpopular due to similar size of quarter; discontinued in 1981.

DATE	Mintages in 1000's	Unc.	Proof
S238 □ 1979P	360,222	2	
S239 □ 1979D	288,016	2	
S240 □ 1979S	109,576	2	10
S241 □ 1979S*			132
S242 □ 1980P	27,610	2	
S243 □ 1980D	41,629	2	
S244 □ 1980S	20,422	3	6
S245 □ 1981P	3,000	6	
S246 □ 1981D	3,250	6	
S247 □ 1981S	7,555	6	6
S248 □ 1981S **			45

*Type 2 (Clear S) **Type 2 (New Clear S)

SILVER DOLLARS
TRADE DOLLAR,
1873-1878

Mint Mark
is Below Eagle
on Reverse

Authorized by Congress Feb. 12, 1873 for use as trade coins in the Orient. Weight and fineness were included in the design to facilitate their circulation among people who were largely unfamiliar with American coinage. Many are found stamped with Chinese characters (chop-marked), indicating they were tested and authenticated by some Chinese merchant. These are usually worth about half the normal price.

DATE	Mintages in 1000's	A.D.P. (VF)	V.Fine	Ex.Fine	AU	Unc.	Proof
TD1 ☐1873	397	55	95	160	275	700	1,700
TD3 ☐1873CC	124	55	95	160	275	700	
TD2 ☐1873S	703	55	90	160	275	700	
TD4 ☐1874	988	50	80	145	275	600	1,700
TD6 ☐1874CC	1,373	55	95	160	275	700	
TD5 ☐1874S	2,549	50	85	145	275	600	
TD7 ☐1875	219	55	150	250	600	1,100	1,700
TD10 ☐1875CC	1,574	50	85	150	375	1,100	
TD8 ☐1875S	4,487	50	85	150	275	600	
TD11 ☐1876	456	50	80	150	275	700	1,700
TD14 ☐1876CC	509	55	95	160	375	1,100	
TD12 ☐1876S	5,227	50	80	145	350	600	
TD15 ☐1877	3,040	50	80	150	350	600	1,700
TD17 ☐1877CC	534	70	125	200	400	1,100	
TD16 ☐1877S	9,519	50	80	150	275	600	
TD20 ☐1878CC	97	125	225	475	1,900	3,000	
TD19 ☐1878S	4,162	50	80	145	275	600	

GOLD DOLLARS, 1849-1852

The smallest of U.S. coins, the gold dollar was designed by James Longacre. Coins minted between 1849 and 1854 weigh 25.8 grains, measure ½ inch in diameter. Minting started concurrent with the gold rush of 1849, California supplying the metal from which these coins were made.

LIBERTY HEAD WITH CORONET, SMALL SIZE
1849-1854
TYPE I

Mint Mark is below wreath on Reverse

	DATE	Mintages in 1000's	A.D.P. (VF)	F.Fine	Ex.Fine	AU	Unc.
G2	☐1849 all kinds	689	150	200	225	275	700
G6	☐1849C. cl. wreath	12	200	300	450	650	1,800
G7	☐1849D op. wreath	22	150	200	250	600	1,700
G8	☐1849 0 op. wreath	215	150	200	225	275	700
G9	☐1850	482	150	200	225	275	700
G10	☐1850C	7	200	300	500	625	2,000
G11	☐1850D	8	200	300	525	650	2,200
G12	☐1850 0	14	150	200	250	300	750
G13	☐1851	3,318	150	200	225	275	700
G14	☐1851C	41	200	300	500	600	1,200
G15	☐1851D	10	200	300	500	650	1,500
G16	☐1851 0	290	150	200	225	275	700
G17	☐1852	2,045	150	200	225	275	700
G18	☐1852C	9	200	275	350	500	1,500
G19	☐1852D	6	200	300	375	600	1,750
G20	☐1852 0	140	150	200	250	325	800

GOLD DOLLARS - LIBERTY HEAD WITH CORONET, SMALL SIZE 1853-1854

DATE	Mintages in 1000's	A.D.P. (VF)	V.Fine	Ex.Fine	AU	Unc.
G21 ☐ 1853	4,076	150	200	225	275	700
G22 ☐ 1853C	12	200	250	450	600	1,500
G23 ☐ 1853D	7	225	275	500	650	1,750
G24 ☐ 1853 O	290	150	200	225	275	700
G25 ☐ 1854.....................	1,636*	150	200	225	275	700
G26 ☐ 1854D	3	275	350	750	1,500	3,500
G27 ☐ 1854S	15	225	275	400	850	2,000

*Includes Indian Headdress Type II of 1854 Type

GOLD DOLLARS - INDIAN HEAD, FEATHER HEADDRESS, LARGE SIZE, 1854-1856 TYPE II

Size increased by 1/16" to 9/16" in diameter. Struck on a slightly thinner planchet it weighs the same.

Mint Mark is Below Wreath on Reverse

DATE	Mintages in 1000's	A.D.P. (VF)	V.Fine	Ex.Fine	AU	Unc.
G28 ☐ 1854.....................	1,636*	250	325	525	900	2,350
G29 ☐ 1855.....................	758	250	325	525	900	2,350
G30 ☐ 1855C	9	375	450	900	2,000	7,500
G31 ☐ 1855D	2	1,750	3,000	4,500	6,000	10,000
G32 ☐ 1855 O	55	325	400	950	1,500	6,000
G38 ☐ 1856S	25	300	375	850	1,300	5,000

*Includes CORONET TYPE I

GOLD DOLLARS
LARGE LIBERTY HEAD, FEATHER HEADDRESS 1856-1865

TYPE III

(Mint Mark is Below Wreath on Reverse)

DATE	Mintages in 1000's	A.D.P. (VF)	V.Fine	Ex.Fine	AU	Unc.	Proof
G34 ☐ 1856 upright 5	33	140	195	220	250	675	
G35 ☐ 1856 slant 5	1,763	140	195	220	250	675	4,000
G36 ☐ 1856D	1	2,000	3,000	4,000	6,000	15,000	
G37 ☐ 1857	775	140	195	220	250	675	4,000
G38 ☐ 1857C	13	275	425	525	800	2,000	
G39 ☐ 1857D	4	275	500	800	1,500	3,500	
G40 ☐ 1857S	10	140	195	350	550	2,000	
G41 ☐ 1858	118	140	195	220	250	675	4,000
G42 ☐ 1858D	3	350	650	900	1,400	3,750	
G43 ☐ 1858S	10	140	195	350	550	1,750	
G44 ☐ 1859	168	140	195	220	250	675	3,500
G45 ☐ 1859C	5	250	350	600	1,000	2,500	
G46 ☐ 1859D	5	275	425	700	1,100	3,000	
G47 ☐ 1859S	15	140	195	350	500	1,500	
G48 ☐ 1860	37	140	195	220	250	675	1,900
G49 ☐ 1860D	2	1,250	2,200	4,000	7,000	12,000	
G50 ☐ 1860S	13	140	195	350	550	1,500	
G52 ☐ 1861	527	140	195	220	250	675	1,900
G53 ☐ 1861D		3,000	4,500	7,000	11,500	21,000	
G54 ☐ 1862	1,327	140	195	220	250	695	1,900
G55 ☐ 1863	6	140	195	325	850	3,750	2,500
G56 ☐ 1864	6	200	300	400	300	3,000	2,500
G57 ☐ 1865	4	200	300	400	800	3,000	2,500

DATE	Mintages in 1000's	A.D.P. (VF)	V.Fine	Ex.Good	AU	Unc.	Proof
G58 ☐ 1866	7	140	195	250	650	2,000	3,000
G59 ☐ 1867	5	140	195	250	700	2,500	3,000
G60 ☐ 1868	11	140	195	250	600	1,750	3,000
G61 ☐ 1869	6	140	195	250	650	1,500	3,000
G62 ☐ 1870	6	140	195	250	600	1,500	3,000
G63 ☐ 1870S	3	225	350	500	900	3,000	—
G64 ☐ 1871	14	140	195	250	600	1,500	3,000
G65 ☐ 1872	4	140	195	250	600	1,600	3,000
G67 ☐ 1873 open 3	125	140	195	325	250	675	
G66 ☐ 1873 closed 3		140	195	325	250	675	3,500
G68 ☐ 1874	199	140	195	225	250	675	4,000
G69 ☐ 1875	(420)*	900	1,300	2,750	3,800	5,000	12,500
G70 ☐ 1876	3	140	195	250	400	1,250	3,500
G71 ☐ 1877	4	140	195	250	350	1,400	3,500
G72 ☐ 1878	3	140	195	250	350	1,250	3,500
G73 ☐ 1879	3	140	195	250	350	1,250	3,500
G74 ☐ 1880	2	140	195	250	350	1,000	3,500
G75 ☐ 1881	7	140	195	225	275	675	1,900
G76 ☐ 1882	5	140	195	225	275	675	1,900
G77 ☐ 1883	11	140	195	225	275	675	1,900
G78 ☐ 1884	6	140	195	225	275	675	1,900
G79 ☐ 1885	12	140	195	225	275	675	1,900
G80 ☐ 1886	6	140	195	225	275	675	1,900
G81 ☐ 1887	9	140	195	225	275	675	1,900
G82 ☐ 1888	16	140	195	225	275	675	1,900
G83 ☐ 1889	31	140	195	225	275	675	1,900

*Total Mintage.

QUARTERS EAGLES ($2.50 GOLD PIECES) 1796-1929

Authorized by the Mint Act in 1792 but first issued in 1796, at a weight of 67½ grains, 13/16" diameter. In 1834 weight was reduced to 64½ grains, diameter to 11/16".

LIBERTY HEAD (Facing Right) 1796-1807

1976 No Stars   1797-1807 With Stars   1796-1807

DATE	Mintages in Full	A.D.P. (F)	Fine	V.Fine	Ex.Fine	AU	Unc.
GH1 ☐1796 no stars	963	6,500	60,000	17,000	27,500	39,000	45,000
GH2 ☐1796 with stars	432	4,000	5,000	10,000	15,000	18,500	40,000
GH3 ☐1797...............	427	3,000	4,000	6,500	9,750	11,000	20,000
GH4 ☐1798...............	1,094	2,500	3,500	5,500	7,500	10,500	17,500
GH6 ☐1802 over 1	3,033	1,950	2,900	4,200	6,300	9,900	16,000
GH7 ☐1804...............	3,237	1,950	2,900	4,200	6,300	9,900	16,000
GH9 ☐1805...............	1,781	1,950	2,900	4,200	6,300	9,900	16,000
GH10☐1806 over 4		1,950	2,900	4,200	6,300	9,900	16,000
GH11☐1806 over 5	1,616	1,950	2,900	4,200	6,500	10,250	17,500
GH12☐1807...............	6,812	1,950	2,900	4,200	6,300	9,900	16,000

LIBERTY HEAD (Facing Left), 1808-1834

1808
Draped Bust
Round Cap

1821-1834
Undraped Liberty
Reduced Size

1808-1834
Motto
Over Eagle

QUARTER EAGLES - LIBERTY HEAD (Facing Left) 1808-1834

DATE	Mintages in 1000's	A.D.P. (F)	Fine	V.Fine	Ex.Fine	AU	Unc.
GH13□1808	2	6,250	9,000	13,500	19,500	29,000	45,000
GH14□1821	6	2,250	3,750	5,000	7,000	9,750	18,000
GH15□1824 over 21	2	2,250	3,750	5,000	7,000	9,750	17,000
GH16□1825	4	2,250	3,750	5,000	7,000	9,750	17,000
GH17□1826 over 25	760*	3,000	4,500	7,000	9,000	15,000	26,000
GH18□1827	2	2,250	3,750	5,000	7,000	10,000	18,000
GH19□1829	3	2,250	3,750	5,000	7,000	9,750	16,000
GH20□1830	4	2,250	3,750	5,000	7,000	9,750	16,000
GH21□1831	4	2,250	3,750	5,000	7,000	9,750	16,000
GH22□1832	4	2,250	3,750	5,000	7,000	9,750	16,000
GH23□1833	4	2,250	3,750	5,000	7,000	9,750	17,000
GH24□1834 motto	4	2,500	4,250	9,500	9,000	12,000	24,000

QUARTER EAGLES ($2.50 Gold Pieces)
LIBERTY HEAD WITH RIBBON, NO MOTTO OVER EAGLE, 1834-1839

Mint Mark is above date on Obverse

DATE	Mintages in 1000's	A.D.P. (VF)	V.Fine	Ex.Fine	AU	Unc.
GH26□1834 no motto	112	200	275	400	800	1,675
GH27□1835	131	200	275	400	800	1,675
GH28□1836	547	200	275	400	800	1,675
GH31□1837	45	200	275	400	800	1,675

*Total mintage

QUARTER EAGLES
LIBERTY HEAD WITH RIBBON, NO MOTTO OVER EAGLE 1838-1839

DATE	Mintages in 1000's	A.D.P. (VF)	Fine	V.Fine	Ex.Fine	AU	Unc.
GH32☐1838	47	200		275	400	800	1,675
GH33☐1838C	8	375		500	1,100	1,500	5,000
GH34☐1839	27	200		275	400	800	1,675
GH36☐1839C	18	200		275	400	800	1,675
GH37☐1839D	14	200		275	400	800	1,675
GH38☐1839 0	18	200		275	400	800	1,675

LIBERTY HEAD WITH CORONET, 1840-1907

Mint Mark is below eagle on Reverse

DATE	Mintages in 1000's	A.D.P. (VF)	V.Fine	Ex.Fine	AU	Unc.
GH39☐1840	19	150	220	275	350	650
GH40☐1840C	13	200	350	500	850	2,200
GH41☐1840D	4	200	475	1,100	2,200	4,500
GH42☐1840 0	26	150	220	275	350	650
GH43☐1841		PROOF ONLY			40,000	60,000
GH44☐1841C	10	200	325	550	700	1,300
GH45☐1841D	4	200	500	1,000	1,500	2,500
GH46☐1842	3	200	425	925	1,400	2,600
GH47☐1842C	7	200	400	750	875	1,900
GH48☐1842D	5	200	500	1,300	1,500	2,400
GH49☐1842 0	20	150	220	275	350	650
GH50☐1843	101	150	220	275	350	650

DATE	Mintages in 1000's	A.D.P. (VF)	V.Fine	Ex.Fine	AU	Unc.
GH51☐1843C small date.........		600	1,000	2,200	2,750	7,000
GH52☐1843C large date	26	200	350	550	850	1,300
GH53☐1843D	36	300	525	800	1,250	2,300
GH55☐1843 O small date	368	150	220	275	300	650
GH56☐1843 O large date.........	-	150	220	275	300	650
GH57☐1844.....................	7	200	325	550	800	1,900
GH58☐1844C	12	200	325	500	700	1,900
GH59☐1844D	17	300	500	900	1,250	2,200
GH60☐1845.....................	91	150	220	275	300	650
GH61☐1845D	19	300	500	900	1,250	2,300
GH62☐1845 O	4	400	750	1,250	1,500	2,900
GH63☐1846.....................	22	150	220	275	300	650
GH64☐1846C	5	325	600	800	1,100	2,150
GH65☐1846D	19	300	500	900	1,300	2,200
GH66☐1846 O	66	150	220	275	300	900
GH67☐1847.....................	30	150	220	275	300	650
GH68☐1847C	23	200	325	500	750	1,400
GH69☐1847D	16	325	550	900	1,300	2,200
GH70☐1847 O	124	150	220	275	300	900
GH71☐1848.....................	7	275	475	775	1,100	1,700
GH72 ☐1848*..................	1	2,750	4,500	7,000	12,500	17,500
GH73☐1848C	17	200	325	500	800	1,300
GH74☐1848D	14	325	550	1,000	1,400	2,400
GH75☐1849.....................	23	150	220	275	300	650
GH76☐1849C	10	200	325	525	775	1,900
GH77☐1849D	11	325	550	900	1,300	2,400
GH78☐1850.....................	253	200	250	300	350	650

*"CAL." above eagle. Gold provided by Col. R.B. Mason. 2 proofs known.

DATE	Mintages in 1000's	A.D.P. (VF)	V.Fine	Ex.Fine	AU	Unc.
GH79 ☐1850C	9	200	325	500	700	1,500
GH80 ☐1850D	12	325	550	900	1,300	2,300
GH81 ☐1850 0	84	150	220	275	300	800
GH82 ☐1851	1,372	150	220	250	290	650
GH83 ☐1851C	15	200	325	475	750	1,300
GH84 ☐1851D	11	325	550	900	1,300	2,300
GH85 ☐1851 0	148	150	220	275	300	700
GH87 ☐1852	1,160	150	220	250	300	650
GH88 ☐1852C	10	200	325	550	775	1,300
GH89 ☐1852D	4	400	650	1,300	1,900	3,400
GH90 ☐1852 0	140	150	220	275	300	700
GH91 ☐1853	1,405	150	220	250	290	650
GH93 ☐1853D	3	400	650	1,200	1,800	2,950
GH94 ☐1854	596	150	220	275	300	650
GH95 ☐1854C	7	200	325	525	775	1,350
GH96 ☐1854D	2	1,250	2,100	4,000	4,750	6,300
GH97 ☐1854 0	15	150	220	275	300	650
GH98 ☐1854S	(246)*		18,000	37,500		
GH99 ☐1855	235	150	220	275	300	650
GH100☐1855C	4	500	800	1,150	1,650	3,200
GH101☐1855D	1	2,000	3,000	4,000	4,300	6,500
GH102☐1856**	384	150	220	275	300	800
GH103☐1856C	8	200	400	550	800	1,750
GH104☐1856D	(874)*	3,500	5,500	9,000	11,000	15,000
GH105☐1856 0	21	170	240	300	400	1,150
GH106☐1856S	72	150	220	300	360	950
GH107☐1857	214	150	220	275	300	650
GH108☐1857D	2	425	750	1,300	2,000	4,500

*Total mintage

** PROOF. STACK SALE 1977   17,000

DATE	Mintages in 1000's	A.D.P. (VF)	V.Fine	Ex.Fine	AU	Unc.	Proof
GH109□1857 O	34	150	220	275	300	700	
GH110□1857S	69	150	220	275	475	1,450	
GH111□1858	47	150	220	275	300	650	22,000
GH112□1858C	9	200	350	500	750	1,400	
GH113□1859	39	150	220	275	325	700	10,000
GH114□1859D	2	500	900	1,300	1,800	3,200	
GH115□1859S	15	150	220	275	425	750	
GH116□1860	23	150	220	275	325	650	5,000
GH117□1860C	7	200	350	600	950	1,850	
GH118□1860S	36	150	220	275	325	700	
GH119□1861	1,273	150	220	275	300	650	5,000
GH120□1861S	24	175	240	290	400	700	
GH122□1862	99	150	220	275	300	650	5,000
GH123□1862S	8	150	220	350	475	1,000	
GH124□1863	(30)*		PROOF ONLY				36,000
GH125□1863S	11	150	220	275	300	650	
GH126□1864	3	600	950	1,900	2,000	3,500	8,000
GH127□1865	2	500	900	1,800	2,000	3,250	8,000
GH128□1865S	23	150	220	275	300	650	
GH129□1866	3	200	275	475	650	1,250	6,000
GH130□1866S	40	150	220	275	325	650	
GH131□1867	3	175	250	425	575	1,300	5,000
GH132□1867S	28	150	220	275	325	650	
GH133□1868	4	200	275	375	575	1,400	5,500
GH134□1868S	34	150	220	300	375	650	
GH135□1869	4	150	225	325	400	1,050	5,000
GH136□1869S	29	150	220	275	300	750	
GH137□1870	5	150	225	335	400	1,050	5,000

*Total mintage

DATE	Mintages in 1000's	A.D.P. (VF)	V.Fine	Ex.Fine	AU	Unc.	Proof
GH138☐1870S	16	150	220	275	300	650	
GH139☐1871...............	5	175	250	300	375	1,200	4,500
GH140☐1871S	22	150	225	275	300	650	
GH141☐1872...............	3	175	250	275	550	1,200	4,500
GH142☐1872S	18	150	225	275	300	650	
GH143☐1873...............	178	Both types			300	650	4,500
GH145☐1873S	27	150	225	275	300	650	
GH146☐1874...............	4	175	275	350	475	900	5,500
GH147☐1875...............	(420)*	1,750	3,000	5,500	7,000	9,000	17,000
GH148☐1875S	12	150	225	275	300	700	
GH149☐1876...............	4	150	225	275	425	1,750	4,500
GH150☐1876S	5	150	225	300	400	1,000	
GH151☐1877...............	2	275	450	700	900	2,000	6,000
GH152☐1877S	35				300	650	
GH153☐1878...............	286				300	650	5,000
GH154☐1878S	178				300	650	
GH155☐1879...............	89				300	650	3,500
GH156☐1879S	43				300	650	
GH157☐1880...............	3	150	225	300	400	800	3,500
GH158☐1881...............	(691)*	450	800	1,200	1,500	3,500	8,800
GH159☐1882...............	4	150	220	295	325	700	3,000
GH160☐1883...............	2	150	225	375	450	800	3,500
GH161☐1884...............	2	150	225	375	450	800	3,500
GH162☐1885...............	(870)*	400	800	1,200	1,500	3,000	7,750
GH163☐1886...............	4				325	650	1,950

*Total mintage

PLEASE NOTE: Unpriced quarter eagles are not considered numismatic items in less than AU condition. and generally bring about 30-50 times face value.

QUARTER EAGLES ($2.50 Gold Piece)
LIBERTY HEAD WITH CORONET 1887-1907

DATE	Mintages in 1000's	A.D.P. (VF)	V.Fine	Ex.Fine	AU	Unc.	Proof
GH164☐1887...............	6				300	650	1,950
GH165☐1888...............	16				300	650	1,950
GH166☐1889...............	17				300	650	2,150
GH167☐1890...............	9				300	650	1,950
GH168☐1891...............	11				300	650	1,950
GH169☐1892...............	2				350	750	1,950
GH170☐1893...............	30				300	650	1,950
GH171☐1894...............	4				350	750	1,950
GH172☐1895...............	6				300	650	1,950
GH173☐1896...............	19				300	650	1,950
GH174☐1897...............	29				300	650	1,950
GH175☐1898...............	24				300	650	1,950
GH176☐1899...............	27				300	650	1,950
GH177☐1900...............	67				300	650	1,950
GH178☐1901...............	91				300	650	1,950
GH179☐1902...............	133				300	650	1,950
GH180☐1903...............	201				300	650	1,950
GH181☐1904...............	160				300	650	1,950
GH182☐1905...............	217				300	650	1,950
GH183☐1906...............	176				300	650	1,950
GH184☐1907...............	336				300	650	1,950

See note on bottom of page 134.

QUARTER EAGLES ($2.50 Gold Pieces)

INDIAN HEAD 1908-1929

These, and the $5 piece of similar dates are unique in U.S. coinage, the designs being incuse, rather than raised. Proofs are granular rather than mirror-like, this type being called matte-proof.

Mint Mark is to left of value on Reverse.

DATE	Mintages in 1000's	A.D.P. (EF)	Ex.Fine	AU	Unc.	Proof
GH185☐1908	565			215	315	2,900
GH186☐1909	442			215	315	2,900
GH187☐1910	493			215	325	2,900
GH188☐1911	704			215	315	2,900
GH189☐1911D	56	515	900	1,000	2,500	
GH190☐1912	616			215	315	2,900
GH191☐1913	722			215	315	2,900
GH192☐1914	240			215	475	2,900
GH193☐1914D	448			215	315	
GH194☐1915	606			215	315	2,900
GH195☐1925D	578			215	315	
GH196☐1926	446			215	315	
GH197☐1927	338			215	315	
GH198☐1928	416			215	315	
GH199☐1929	432			215	315	

Coins in less than AU conditon generally bring about 30-50 times face value.

$3.00 GOLD PIECES
LIBERTY HEAD WITH FEATHER HEADDRESS 1854-1863

Similar in design to the $1, both having been designed by James Longacre. Not many were minted due to indifferent response by the public. Weight 77.4 grains, diameter 13/16''.

Mint Mark is below wreath on Reverse

	DATE	Mintages in 1000's	A.D.P. (VF)	V.Fine	Ex.Fine	AU	Unc.	Proof
GT1	☐1854	137	400	550	800	1,000	2,400	4,000
GT2	☐1854D	1	5,000	8,000	13,000	19,000	72,500	
GT3	☐1854 O	24	400	550	1,100	1,500	2,650	
GT4	☐1855	51	400	550	800	1,000	2,400	35,000
GT5	☐1855S	6	500	750	1,400	2,200		
GT6	☐1856	26	400	550	800	1,000	2,600	21,000
GT7	☐1856S	34	500	750	950	1,500	3,100	
GT10	☐1857	21	400	550	800	1,000	2,400	17,000
GT11	☐1857S	14	500	750	1,100	1,900	4,000	
GT12	☐1858	2	500	800	1,300	2,300	2,850	14,000
GT13	☐1859	16	400	550	800	1,000	2,400	14,000
GT14	☐1860	7	500	750	1,000	1,500	2,500	14,000
GT15	☐1860S	7	500	750	1,050	1,750	4,500	
GT16	☐1861	6	475	725	1,050	1,500	2,850	11,000
GT17	☐1862	6	475	725	1,050	1,400	2,950	11,000
GT18	☐1863	5	500	750	1,050	1,500	2,950	11,000

$3.00 GOLD PIECES (Cont'd.) —
LIBERTY HEAD WITH FEATHER HEADDRESS 1864-1889

DATE	Mintages in 1000's	A.D.P. (VF)	V.Fine	Ex.Fine	AU	Unc.	Proof
GT19☐1864	3	500	750	1,100	1,500	3,100	9,000
GT20☐1865	1	600	800	1,100	1,500	4,850	10,000
GT21☐1866	4	500	750	1,100	1,500	3,000	10,000
GT22☐1867	3	600	800	1,100	1,500	3,000	10,000
GT23☐1868	5	500	750	1,075	1,400	2,900	10,000
GT24☐1869	3	500	750	1,100	1,500	3,200	10,000
GT25☐1870	4	500	750	950	1,350	3,000	7,000
GT26☐1870S		Only two known. 1982 Auction 687,500.					
GT27☐1871	1	650	875	1,100	1,500	2,900	7,000
GT28☐1872	2	600	800	1,100	1,500	2,850	7,000
GT29☐1873 open 3	(25)	Proof only					35,000
☐1873 closed 3 First restrike	(20)**	Proof only					40,000
☐1873 closed 3 Second restrike	(200)**		4,000	5,000	5,500	10,500	12,500
GT30☐1874	42	400	550	800	1,000	2,400	7,000
GT31☐1875	(20)*	Proof only 1982 Auction					62,500
GT32☐1876	(45)*	Proof only					16,000
GT33☐1877	1	750	900	1,500	2,250	3,550	10,000
GT34☐1878	82	400	550	800	1,000	2,400	9,500
GT35☐1879	3	475	675	900	1,100	2,450	6,500
GT36☐1880	1	525	825	1,100	1,500	2,600	6,000
GT37☐1881	(550)*	550	850	1,500	1,800	2,950	6,500
GT38☐1882	2	600	800	1,025	1,300	2,650	5,500
GT39☐1883	1	600	800	1,025	1,300	2,750	4,500
GT40☐1884	1	600	800	1,100	1,400	2,650	4,500
GT41☐1885	1	675	875	1,150	1,600	3,450	4,500
GT42☐1886	1	625	825	1,200	1,600	2,600	4,500
GT43☐1887	6	425	625	900	1,050	2,400	4,500
GT44☐1889	2	425	625	900	1,050	2,450	4,500
GT45☐1889	2	425	625	900	1,050	2,450	4,500

*Full mintage **unofficial full mintage

4 DOLLAR GOLD OR STELLA
LIBERTY HEAD WITH FLOWING OR COILED HAIR 1879-1880

Actually patterns not minted for general circulation, these were designed by Charles E. Barber and George T. Morgan and called Stellas because of the star.

DATE	Mintages in Full	Proof
☐1879 flowing hair	415	40,000
☐1879 coiled hair	10	100,000
☐1880 flowing hair	15	*65,000
☐1880 coiled hair	10	*100,000

HALF EAGLES ($5.00 Gold Pieces) 1795-1929

The half eagle has the distinction of being the first gold coin struck under the 1792 Mint Act; also the only U.S. coin struck in all seven mints. Early coins, 1795-1834, weigh 135 grains, .916-2/3 fine; 1834 to 1837, 129 grains, 899.225 fine; 1837 on, 129 grains .900 fine. In 1834 size reduced from 1 inch to 7/8 inch in diameter.

1795-1807   1795-1798 Small Eagle   1795-1807 Large Eagle

HALF EAGLES - ($5.00 Gold Pieces) 1795-1807

DATE	Mintages in 1000's	A.D.P. (VF)	V.Fine	Ex.Fine	AU	Unc.
GF1 □1795 sm. Eagle	9	4,000	6,000	8,500	10,000	20,000
GF6 □1795 lg. Eagle	9	6,000	9,000	11,750	13,000	26,500
GF2 □1796	6	6,000	9,000	11,750	13,000	26,500
GF3 □1797	4	6,000	9,000	11,750	13,000	26,500
GF5 □1798 sm. Eagle		7 KNOWN 1982 Auction VF 70,000				
GF9 □1798 lg. Eagle	25	1,100	1,700	2,900	4,950	10,700
GF12□1799	7	1,100	1,700	2,900	4,950	10,700
GF16□1800	38	1,100	1,700	2,900	4,950	10,700
GF17□1802 over 1	53	1,100	1,700	2,900	4,950	10,700
GF18□1803 over 2	34	1,100	1,700	2,900	4,950	10,700
GF19□1804	30	1,100	1,700	2,900	4,950	10,700
GF21□1805	33	1,100	1,700	2,900	4,950	10,700
GF22□1806	64	1,100	1,700	2,900	4,950	10,700
GF24□1807	33	1,100	1,700	2,900	4,950	10,700

HALF EAGLES - ($5.00 Gold Pieces)
DRAPED BUST, VALUE 5D ON REVERSE 1807-1812

DATE	Mintages in 1000's	A.D.P. (VF)	V.Fine	Ex.Fine	AU	Unc.
GF27□1807	51	950	1,650	2,400	4,200	10,175
GF28□1808	56	950	1,650	2,400	4,200	10,175
GF30□1809	34	950	1,650	2,400	4,200	10,175
GF31□1810*	100	950	1,650	2,400	4,200	10,175
GF35□1811	100	950	1,650	2,400	4,200	10,175
GF37□1812	58	950	1,650	2,400	4,200	10,175

*Large and small date with small 5. rare.

HALF EAGLES ($5.00 Gold Pieces)
LIBERTY HEAD, ROUND CAP, MOTTO OVER EAGLE 1813-1834

DATE	Mintages in 1000's	A.D.P. (VF)	V.Fine	Ex.Fine	AU	Unc.
GF38☐1813........................	95	1,000	2,000	3,200	6,250	12,500
GF39☐1814........................	15	1,000	2,000	3,200	6,250	12,500
GF40☐1815........................	1		1979 AUCTION			150,000
GF41☐1818........................	49	1,000	2,000	3,200	6,250	12,500
GF43☐1819........................	52				12,000	32,500
GF45☐1820........................	264	1,000	2,000	3,200	6,250	12,500
GF48☐1821........................	35	2,250	4,500	7,000	9,000	14,500
GF49☐1822........................		3 KNOWN 1982 AUCTION VF				687,500
GF50☐1823........................	14	1,400	2,500	4,000	6,250	14,500
GF51☐1824........................	17	4,000	8,000	11,250	16,000	32,000
GF52☐1825 over 21	29	2,500	5,000	7,500	9,000	15,000
GF54☐1826........................	18	3,000	6,000	8,500	10,000	19,000
GF55☐1827........................	25			15,000	RARE	40,000
GF57☐1828........................	28		1982 AUCTION AU			40,000
GF59☐1829 small date	57		1982 AUCTION UNC			75,000
GF58☐1829 large date			1982 AUCTION EF			26,000
GF60☐1830........................	126	2,700	5,350	8,500	11,275	19,750
GF62☐1831........................	141	2,700	5,350	8,500	11,275	19,750
GF64☐1832........................	157	2,700	5,350	8,500	11,275	21,000
GF65☐1833........................	194	2,700	5,350	8,500	11,275	19,750
GF67☐1834........................	50	2,700	5,350	8,500	11,275	19,750

HALF EAGLES ($5.00 Gold Pieces)
LIBERTY HEAD WITH RIBBON, NO MOTTO OVER EAGLE 1834-1838

Mint mark is Above
Date on Obverse

DATE	Mintages in 1000's	A.D.P. (VF)	V.Fine	Ex.Fine	AU	Unc.
GF69 ☐ 1834 plain 4	657	200	290	415	900	2,200
GF70 ☐ 1834 crosslet 4	682	350	900	1,000	1,500	
GF71 ☐ 1835	372	200	290	415	900	2,200
GF72 ☐ 1836	553	200	290	415	900	2,200
GF73 ☐ 1837	207	200	290	415	900	2,200
GF76 ☐ 1838	287	200	290	415	900	2,200
GF78 ☐ 1838 C	17	550	1,000	1,750	2,500	6,000
GF79 ☐ 1838 D	21	550	1,000	1,900	3,000	8,000

LIBERTY HEAD WITH CORONET 1839-1908

1839-1908   1839-66 No Motto   1866-1908 With Motto
(Mint Mark is Below Eagle on Reverse)

HALF EAGLES ($5.00 Gold Pieces)
LIBERTY HEAD WITH CORONET 1839-1847

DATE	Mintages in 1000's	A.D.P. (VF)	V.Fine	Ex.Fine	AU	Unc.
GH80 ☐1839.....................	118	180	225	325	500	1,800
GH82 ☐1839C	17	225	450	750	1,000	2,500
GH83 ☐1839D	19	300	525	1,150	2,000	5,000
GH84 ☐1840.....................	137	180	225	325	500	825
GH85 ☐1840C	19	225	350	550	900	1,950
GH86 ☐1840D	23	300	525	850	1,250	5,000
GH87 ☐1840 O	40	180	230	325	500	5,500
GH88 ☐1841.....................	16	180	225	325	500	1,800
GH89 ☐1841C	22	225	350	550	750	1,950
GH90 ☐1841D	30	275	475	750	1,000	4,500
GH91 ☐1841 O		2 KNOWN				
GH92 ☐1842.....................	28	180	230	325	500	1,800
GH94 ☐1842C	27	225	350	600	800	2,200
GH95 ☐1842D sm. date..........	60	250	450	725	875	4,500
GH98 ☐1842 O.................	16	200	300	550	750	1,800
GH99 ☐1843.....................	611	180	210	225	360	825
GH100☐1843C	44	225	325	500	750	1,850
GH101☐1843D	98	250	450	725	875	4,500
GH103☐1843 O sm. letters	101	180	230	325	500	1,800
GH105☐1844.....................	340	180	210	225	360	825
GH106☐1844C	24	225	325	550	700	2,200
GH107☐1844D	89	300	500	600	850	4,500
GH108☐1844 O.................	365	180	210	225	360	825
GH109☐1845.....................	417	180	210	225	360	825
GH110☐1845D	90	250	450	600	850	4,500
GH111☐1845 O.................	41	180	230	300	550	1,800
GH112☐1846.....................	396	180	210	325	360	825
GH114☐1847C	13	300	500	700	900	2,200
GH115☐1847D	80	225	450	600	800	4,500
GH116☐1847 O.................	58	180	230	300	550	1,800
GH117☐1847.....................	916	180	210	225	360	825

DATE	Mintages in 1000's	A.D.P. (F)	Good	Fine	V.Fine	E.Fine
GF118☐1847C	84	225	350	600	800	1,950
GF119☐1847D	64	300	500	875	1,000	4,500
GF120☐1847 O................	12	225	400	750	900	2,000
GF121☐1848................	261	180	210	225	360	1,800
GF122☐1848C	64	225	325	550	750	2,000
GF123☐1848D	47	250	450	875	1,000	5,000
GF124☐1849................	133	180	210	225	360	825
GF125☐1849C	65	225	325	550	750	1,850
GF126☐1849D	39	250	500	1,000	1,200	4,500
GF127☐1850................	65	180	210	270	375	1,800
GF128☐1850C	64	225	325	550	750	1,850
GF129☐1850D	44	300	500	1,000	1,200	4,750
GF130☐1851................	378	180	210	225	360	825
GF131☐1851C	49	225	325	550	750	1,850
GF132☐1851D	63	250	450	600	900	4,500
GF133☐1851 O................	41	180	230	275	375	1,800
GF134☐1852................	574	180	210	225	360	825
GF135☐1852C	73	225	325	600	900	1,800
GF136☐1852D	91	250	450	625	900	4,500
GF137☐1853................	306	180	210	225	360	825
GF138☐1853C	66	225	350	600	900	1,800
GF139☐1853D	90	250	450	600	900	4,500
GF140☐1854................	161	180	210	225	360	825
GF141☐1854C	39	225	325	550	750	1,900
GF142☐1854D	56	250	430	600	900	4,500
GF143☐1854 O................	46	200	250	325	500	1,800
GF144☐1854S	(268)*		1982 AUCTION AU			187,000
GF145☐1855 Proof 12,000		180	210	225	360	825
GF146☐1855C	40	225	325	600	900	1,850

*Total mintage

DATE	Mintages in 1000's	A.D.P. (VF)	V.Fine	Ex.Fine	AU	Unc.	Proof
GF174 □ 1855D	22	250	450	600	900	5,500	
GF148 □ 1855 O	11	250	400	650	900	1,850	
GF149 □ 1855S	61	200	250	375	575	1,800	
GF150 □ 1856	198	180	210	225	360	825	10,000
GF151 □ 1856C	28	225	400	600	900	2,250	
GF152 □ 1856D	20	250	450	675	975	5,500	
GF153 □ 1856 O	10	225	400	800	1,000	1,900	
GF154 □ 1856S	105	180	210	225	360	825	
GF155 □ 1857	98	180	210	225	360	825	10,000
GF156 □ 1857C	17	225	400	600	800	1,850	
GF157 □ 1857D	17	250	450	725	1,000	6,000	
GF158 □ 1857 O	13	200	300	450	600	1,950	
GF159 □ 1857S	87	180	210	225	360	825	
GF160 □ 1858	15	180	230	350	550	1,600	10,000
GF161 □ 1858C	39	225	350	600	800	1,950	
GF162 □ 1858D	15	250	475	875	1,000	6,000	
GF163 □ 1858S	19	180	230	350	500	1,800	
GF164 □ 1859	17	200	275	450	600	1,800	7,500
GF165 □ 1859C	32	225	325	600	800	2,000	
GF166 □ 1859D	10	250	500	675	875	6,000	
GF167 □ 1859S	13	225	350	550	750	1,800	
GF168 □ 1860	20	180	230	275	375	1,800	6,500
GF169 □ 1860C	15	225	400	650	850	2,250	
GF171 □ 1860D	15	300	550	1,200	1,500	6,000	
GF172 □ 1860S	21	200	250	350	500	1,800	
GF173 □ 1861	688	180	210	225	360	825	6,500
GF174 □ 1861C	7	500	800	1,500	1,750	3,000	
GF175 □ 1861D	(1,597)*	2,400	4,300	5,850	7,500	15,000	
GF176 □ 1861S	9	225	350	600	800	RARE IN UNC	

*Total mintage

HALF EAGLES ($5.00 Gold Pieces)
LIBERTY HEAD WITH CORONET 1862-1873 (Cont'd.)

DATE	Mintages in 1000's	A.D.P. (VF)	V.Fine	Ex.Fine	AU	Unc.	Proof
GF177☐1862	4	250	450	650	800	1,800	6,500
GF178☐1862S	9	200	275	500	850	RARE IN UNC	
GF179☐1863	2	400	700	1,300	1,600	3,000	6,500
GF180☐1863S	17	225	350	600	800	RARE IN UNC	
GF181☐1864	4	225	425	550	750	3,500	6,500
GF182☐1864S	4	850	1,500	2,000	2,500	5,000	
GF183☐1865	(1,295)*	400	700	1,400	1,750	3,000	6,500
GF184☐1865S	28	200	300	600	800	RARE IN UNC	
GF185☐1866S	9	200	325	650	850	RARE IN UNC	
MOTTO OVER EAGLE							
GF186☐1866	7	200	300	450	775	1,350	9,000
GF187☐1866S	34	200	300	500	750	1,250	
GF188☐1867	7	200	350	675	800	1,250	9,000
GF189☐1867S	29	200		400	650	RARE IN UNC	
GF190☐1868	6	200	290	600	750	1,950	9,000
GF191☐1868S	52	200		300	450	RARE IN UNC	
GF192☐1869	2	400	625	875	1,750	4,000	9,000
GF193☐1869S	31	200	300	400	500	800	
GF194☐1870	4	200	350	750	1,000	1,250	9,000
GF196☐1880C	7	1,350	2,500	3,800	7,250	UNKNOWN IN UNC	
GF195☐1870S	17	200	300	350	400	800	
GF197☐1871	3	225	375	600	750	1000	9,000
GF200☐1871CC	21	350	500	850	1,200	2,900	
GF198☐1871S	25	200	300	350	500	800	
GF201☐1872	(1,690)*	400	750	1,250	1,500	2,500	9,000
GF203☐1872CC	17	400	725	1,250	1,600	5,000	
GF202☐1872S	36	200		275	325	550	
GF204☐1873	112	180		235	260	395	9,000

*Total mintage

For coins not priced, see note at bottom of page 150.

HALF EAGLES ($5.00 Gold Pieces)
LIBERTY HEAD WITH CORONET 1873-1882 (Cont'd.)
MOTTO OVER EAGLE

DATE	Mintages in 1000's	A.D.P. [F]	Good	V.Good	Fine	V.Fine	E.Fine
GF207☐1873CC	7	400	750	1,350	1,500	2,500	
GF206☐1873S	31	180	225	300	350	650	
GF208☐1874	4	225	400	600	750	1,000	9,000
GF210☐1874CC	21	325	550	775	1,550	3,500	
GF209☐1874S	16	180	225	325	600	RARE IN UNC.	
GF211☐1875	(220)	*Very Rare 1982 Auction				60,000	
GF213☐1875CC	11	550	800	1,250	1,500	3,500	
GF212☐1875S	9	300	500	750	1,000	2,000	
GF214☐1876	(1,477)*	300	500	1,100	1,250	2,250	8,000
GF216☐1876CC	1	300	500	1,100	1,250	2,250	
GF215☐1876S	4	500	1,000	2,100	2,500	RARE IN UNC.	
GF217☐1877	(1,152)*	300	500	1,250	1,500	2,500	9,000
GF219☐1877CC	9	300	500	1,300	1,500	2,750	
GF218☐1877S	27			235	275	450	
GF220☐1878	132				210	275	9,000
GF222☐1878CC	9	900	1,650	2,700	4,500	RARE IN UNC.	
GF221☐1878S	145				210	675	
GF223☐1879	302				210	675	8,000
GF225☐1879CC	17	225	400	550	700	950	
GF224☐1879S	426				210	275	
GF226☐1880	3,166				210	275	7,500
GF228☐1880CC	51	225	400	550	700	950	
GF227☐1880S	1,349				210	275	
GF230☐1881	5,709				210	275	5,500
GF232☐1881CC	14	225	400	550	700	950	
GF231☐1881S	969				210	275	
GF233☐1882	2,515				210	275	5,500
GF235☐1882CC	83	190	250	500	650	950	

*Total mintage
Please note: Unpriced half eagles are not considered numismatic items in less than uncirculated condition, and generally bring about 15-25 times face value.

DATE	Mintages in 1000's	A.D.P. (EF)	Ex.Fine	AU	Unc.	Proof
GF234 □ 1882S	969			210	275	
GF236 □ 1883	233			210	275	5,500
GF238 □ 1883CC	13	225	400	650	950	
GF237 □ 1883S	83			210	275	
GF239 □ 1884	191			210	275	5,500
GF241 □ 1884CC	16	250	500	650	850	
GF240 □ 1884S	177			210	275	
GF242 □ 1885	602			210	275	5,500
GF243 □ 1885S	1,211			210	275	
GF244 □ 1886	388			210	275	5,500
GF245 □ 1886S	3,268			210	275	
GF246 □ 1887	(87)*		PROOF ONLY			22,000
GF247 □ 1887S	1,912			210	275	
GF248 □ 1888	18			210	275	5,500
GF249 □ 1888S	294			210	275	
GF250 □ 1889	8	250	400	550	800	6,000
GF251 □ 1890	4	250	400	550	800	6,000
GF252 □ 1890CC	54	200	500	475	900	
GF253 □ 1891	61			210	275	5,500
GF254 □ 1891CC	208	200	275	425	900	
GF255 □ 1892	754			210	275	5,300
GF258 □ 1892CC	83			450	900	
GF256 □ 1892 O	10	500	725	1,500	2,250	

*Total mintage

See note at bottom of page 150.

HALF EAGLES (5.00 Gold Pieces)
LIBERTY HEAD WITH CORONET 1892-1901 (Cont'd.)
MOTTO OVER EAGLE

DATE	Mintages in 1000's	A.D.P. (EF)	Ex.Fine	AU	Unc.	Proof
GF257 ☐ 1892S	298			280	275	
GF259 ☐ 1893	1,528			280	275	3,050
GF262 ☐ 1893CC	60		275	500	900	
GF260 ☐ 1893 O	110		300	400	700	
GF261 ☐ 1893S	224			210	275	
GF263 ☐ 1894	958			210	275	3,050
GF264 ☐ 1894 O	17		300	400	750	
GF265 ☐ 1894S	56			210	275	
GF266 ☐ 1895	1,346			210	275	3,050
GF267 ☐ 1895S	112			210	275	
GF268 ☐ 1896	59			210	275	3,050
GF269 ☐ 1896S	155			210	275	
GF270 ☐ 1897	868			210	275	3,050
GF271 ☐ 1897S	345			210	275	
GF272 ☐ 1898	633			210	275	3,050
GF273 ☐ 1898S	1,397			210	275	
GF274 ☐ 1899	1,711			210	275	3,050
GF275 ☐ 1899S	1,545			210	275	
GF276 ☐ 1900	1,406			210	275	3,050
GF277 ☐ 1900S	329			210	275	
GF278 ☐ 1901	616			210	275	3,050
GF279 ☐ 1901S	3,648			210	275	
GF280 ☐ 1902	173			210	275	3,050
GF281 ☐ 1902S	939			210	275	

See note at bottom of page 150.

HALF EAGLES ($5.00 Gold Pieces)
LIBERTY HEAD WITH CORONET 1903-1908 (Cont'd.)
MOTTO OVER EAGLE

DATE	Mintages in 1000's	A.D.P. AU	Unc.	Proof
GF282☐1903	227	210	275	3,050
GF283☐1903S	1,855	210	275	
GF284☐1904	392	210	275	3,050
GF285☐1904S	97	290	900	
GF286☐1905	302	210	275	3,050
GF287☐1905S	881	210	275	
GF289☐1906	349	210	275	3,050
GF290☐1906S	598	210	275	
GF291☐1906D	320	210	275	
GF292☐1907	626	210	275	3,050
GF293☐1907D	888	210	275	
GF294☐1908	422	210	275	

HALF EAGLES ($5.00 Gold Pieces)
INDIAN HEAD 1908-1929

(Mint Mark is to Left of Value on Reverse)

HALF EAGLES ($5.00 Gold Pieces)
INDIAN HEAD 1908-1929

DATE	Mintages in 1000's	A.D.P. (EF)	Ex.Fine	AU	Unc.	Proof
GF295☐1908	578			300	950	4.400
GF296☐1908D	148			400	975	
GF297☐1908S	82	300	400	475	2.500	
GF298☐1909	627			300	975	4.400
GF299☐1909 O	34	600	925	1.050	6.900	
GF300☐1909D	3.423			300	950	
GF301☐1909S	297			325	1.550	
GF302☐1910	604			300	975	4.400
GF303☐1910D	194			300	975	
GF304☐1910S	770			325	2.100	
GF305☐1911	915			300	950	4.400
GF306☐1911D	72	325	450	500	4.400	
GF306☐1911S	1.416			325	1.325	
GF308☐1912	790			300	950	4.400
GF309☐1912S	392			325	1.925	
GF310☐1913	916			300	925	4.400
GF311☐1913S	408			375	3.300	
GF312☐1914	247			300	925	4.400
GF313☐1914D	247			300	975	
GF314☐1914S	263			325	1.325	
GF315☐1915	588			300	925	4.500
GF316☐1915S	164			375	2.650	
GF317☐1916S	240			325	1.325	
GF318☐1929	662	2.000	3.500	3.850	5.600	

*AT THIS WRITING. DEALERS ARE PAYING ABOUT 25-30 TIMES FACE VALUE EACH FOR EF COINS OF COMMON DATES.

EAGLES ($10.00 Gold Pieces) 1795-1933

Weight and size — 1795 to 1804: 270 grains, 1-5/16''; 1838 on: 258 grains, 1-1/16''. No denomination appeared until 1838.

LIBERTY HEAD, SMALL EAGLE 1795-1797

DATE	Mintages in 1000's	A.D.P. (F)	Good	V.Good	Fine	V.Fine	E.Fine
GE1 □ 1795	5	3,500	6,500	9,500	13,250	19,250	29,975
GE3 □ 1796	4	3,500	6,500	9,500	13,250	19,250	29,975
GE4 □ 1797	3	3,500	6,500	9,500	13,250	19,250	29,975

LIBERTY HEAD, LARGE EAGLE 1797-1804

EAGLES ($10.00 Gold Pieces)
LIBERTY HEAD LARGE EAGLE 1797-1804

DATE	Mintages in 1000's	A.D.P. (F)	Fine	V.Fine	Ex.Fine	AU	Unc.
GE5 ☐1797...............	11	1,250	2,575	3,595	5,350	7,925	16,500
GE6 ☐1798 8 over 7†	(900)*		1982 AUCTION AU				30,000
GE7 ☐1798 8 over 7††	(842)*		1982 AUCTION EF				46,000
GE8 ☐1799.................	37	1,250	2,575	3,575	5,350	7,925	16,500
GE10☐1800.................	6	1,250	2,575	3,575	5,350	7,925	16,500
GE11☐1801.................	44	1,250	2,575	3,575	5,350	7,925	16,500
GE12☐1803.................	15	1,250	2,575	3,575	5,350	7,925	16,500
GE14☐1804.................	4	1,750	3,000	4,000	6,500	9,000	20,000

*Total Mintage   †9 stars left 4 right   ††7 stars left 6 right

EAGLES ($10.00 Gold Pieces)
LIBERTY HEAD WITH CORONET 1838-1842

1838-1907

1838-1866
No Motto

1866-1907
With Motto

Mint Mark

DATE	Mintages in 1000's	A.D.P. (F)	Fine	V.Fine	Ex.Fine	AU	Unc.
GE15☐1838.................	7	300	395	600	1,100	2,300	7,750
GE17☐1839 Sm. Ltrs.	25	350	500	1,000	1,500	3,200	8,000
GE18☐1839 Lg. Ltrs.	12	300	395	600	1,100	2,700	7,750
GE19☐1840.................	47	275	350	375	450	1,750	4,700
GE20☐1841.................	63	275	350	395	450	1,750	4,700
GE21☐1841 0	2	300	400	650	1,200	2,000	6,500
GE22☐1842.................	82		350	375	450	1,750	4,700

Please note: Unpriced eagles are not considered numismatic items in less than uncirculated condition, and generally bring about 25 times face value.

DATE	Mintages in 1000's	A.D.P. (EF)	Ex.Fine	AU	Proof
GE24 ☐ 1842 0	27	325	450	950	4,700
GE25 ☐ 1843	75	325	450	950	4,700
GE26 ☐ 1843 0	175	325	450	950	3,200
GE27 ☐ 1844	6	325	450	950	5,500
GE28 ☐ 1844 0	119	325	450	950	4,000
GE29 ☐ 1845	26	325	460	1,000	5,500
GE30 ☐ 1845 0	47	325	460	1,000	5,500
GE31 ☐ 1846	20	325	460	1,000	5,500
GE33 ☐ 1846 0	82	325	460	1,000	5,500
GE34 ☐ 1847	862	275	350	480	2,500
GE35 ☐ 1847 0	571	300	410	500	2,900
GE36 ☐ 1848	145	275	350	480	2,500
GE37 ☐ 1848 0	36	325	460	1,000	3,600
GE38 ☐ 1849	653	275	350	480	1,350
GE39 ☐ 1849 0	24	325	460	1,000	3,200
GE40 ☐ 1850	291	275	350	480	1,500
GE41 ☐ 1850 0	57	325	460	1,000	3,500
GE42 ☐ 1851	176	275	350	480	1,500
GE43 ☐ 1851 0	263	275	350	480	1,350
GE44 ☐ 1852	263	325	460	950	2,500
GE45 ☐ 1852 0	18	290	370	500	3,450
GE47 ☐ 1853	201	275	350	480	1,350
GE48 ☐ 1853 0	51	325	460	950	3,300
GE49 ☐ 1854	54	325	460	950	3,300
GE50 ☐ 1854 0	52	325	460	950	3,300
GE52 ☐ 1854S	124	275	350	480	1,350
GE53 ☐ 1855	122	275	350	480	1,350
GE54 ☐ 1855 0	18	325	460	950	3,300
GE55 ☐ 1855S	9	550	1,100	1,800	5,250

DATE	Mintages in 1000's	A.D.P. (EF)	Ex.Fine	AU	Unc.	Proof
GE56☐1856................	60	325	460	850	3.600	25.000
GE57☐1856 O..............	14	325	460	850	3.600	
GE58☐1856S	68	325	460	850	3.150	
GE59☐1857...............	17	325	460	750	3.200	23.000
GE60☐1857 O..............	5	800	1.400	2.300	RARE	
GE61☐1857S	26	325	460	750	2.750	
GE62☐1858...............	3	3.000	5.400	7.400	RARE	23.000
GE63☐1858 O..............	20	325	460	750	2.750	
GE64☐1858S	12	325	460	950	3.200	
GE65☐1859...............	16	325	460	950	2.100	21.000
GE66☐1859 O..............	2	1.800	3.200	4.000	RARE	
GE67☐1859S	7	600	1.150	1.500	3.600	
GE68☐1860...............	15	325	460	750	2.100	15.000
GE69☐1860 O..............	11	450	700	1.000	3.600	
GE70☐1860S	5	650	1.250	1.500	5.500	
GE71☐1861...............	113	275	350	480	1.350	12.500
GE72☐1861S	15	325	500	700	1.950	
GE73☐1862...............	11	275	350	480	1.350	16.000
GE74☐1862S	12	425	825	1.000	3.000	
GE75☐1863...............	(1.248)*	900	1.650	2.950	8.000	15.000
GE76☐1863S	10	550	950	1.250	2.750	
GE77☐1864...............	4	800	1.500	2.000	5.500	15.000
GE78☐1864S	2	1.100	2.000	3.000	6.000	
GE79☐1865...............	4	700	1.250	2.000	5.750	12.000
GE80☐1865S	17	650	1.200	2.000	4.750	
GE82☐1866S no motto	8	1.100	2.000	3.200	RARE	
GE83☐1866 with motto	4	325	500	800	1.200	9.000
GE84☐1866S with motto	12	350	600	850	1.400	
GE85☐1867...............	3	325	500	700	1.100	9.000

*Total mintage

DATE	Mintages in 1000's	A.D.P. (EF)	Ex.Fine	AU	Unc.	Proof
GE86 ☐1867S	9	350	650	800	1,250	
GE87 ☐1868	11	300	400	600	800	6,000
GE88 ☐1868S	13	325	550	650	1,000	
GE89 ☐1869	2	1,350	2,500	3,250	4,000	9,500
GE90 ☐1869S	6	350	650	775	1,350	
GE91 ☐1870	4	475	850	975	1,250	9,500
GE93 ☐1870CC	6	2,500	3,600	8,000	RARE	
GE92 ☐1870S	8	325	600	800	1,200	
GE94 ☐1871	2	1,100	2,250	2,600	3,500	9,500
GE96 ☐1871CC	8	800	1,500	1,750	2,500	
GE95 ☐1871S	16	325	550	650	950	
GE97 ☐1872	2	1,100	2,000	2,650	3,500	8,500
GE99 ☐1872CC	5	575	1,000	1,400	3,100	
GE98 ☐1872S	17	325	500	600	950	
GE100☐1873	(825)*	1,350	2,500	3,250	5,000	12,500
GE102☐1873CC	5	950	1,750	2,800	RARE	
GE101☐1873S	12	325	550	700	1,000	
GE103 ☐1874	53	295	325	395	650	8,500
GE105 ☐1874CC	17	475	900	1,100	1,600	
GE104 ☐1874S	10	350	650	850	1,250	
GE106 ☐1875	(120)*			1982 AUCTION		95,000
GE107☐1875CC	8	700	1,300	1,900	2,500	
GE108☐1876	(732)*	2,250	4,000	5,500	8,500	7,000
GE110☐1876CC	5	850	1,750	2,200	3,500	
GE109☐1876S	5	600	1,000	1,400	2,000	
GE111☐1877	(817)*	2,800	4,500	5,250	7,500	7,000
GE113☐1877CC	3	1,150	2,250	2,750	4,000	
GE112☐1877S	17	300	400	550	650	

*Total mintage

EAGLES ($10.00 Gold Pieces)
LIBERTY HEAD WITH CORONET 1878-1886 (Cont'd.)
MOTTO OVER EAGLE

DATE	Mintages in 1000's	A.D.P. (EF)	Ex.Fine	AU	Unc.	Proof
GE114□1878...................	74			330	375	8,500
GE116□1878CC.................	3	1,150	2,250	2,750	4,000	
GE115□1878S	26	275	350	450	575	
GE117□1879...................	385			330	375	5,000
GE120□1879CC.................	2	3,000	5,650	9,000	RARE	
GE118□1879 0.................	1	1,500	3,100	4,600	6,000	
GE119□1879S	224			330	375	
GE121□1880...................	1,645			330	375	5,000
GE124□1880CC.................	11	400	700	800	1,400	
GE122□1880 0.................	9	350	600	750	1,100	
GE123□1880S	500			330	375	
GE125□1881...................	3,877			330	375	5,000
GE128□1881CC.................	24	325	450	650	1,150	
GE126□1881 0.................	8	325	500	650	900	
GE127□1881S	970			330	375	
GE129□1882...................	2,324			330	375	4,500
GE132□1882CC.................	7	350	550	800	1,600	
GE130□1882 0.................	11	290	365	500	650	
GE131□1882S	132			330	375	
GE133□1883...................	208			330	375	4,500
GE136□1883CC.................	12	400	700	950	1,400	
GE134□1883 0.................	(800)*	1,950	3,850	5,300	9,000	
GE135□1883S	38			330	375	
GE137□1884...................	76			330	375	12,500
GE139□1884CC.................	10	350	550	850	1,400	
GE138□1884S	124			330	375	
GE140□1885...................	254			330	375	4,000
GE141□1885S	228			330	375	
GE142□1886...................	236			330	375	4,000
GE143□1886S	826			330	375	

*Total mintage   See note on bottom of page 156.

DATE	Mintages in 1000's	A.D.P. (EF)	Ex.Fine	AU	Unc.	Proof
GE144☐1887	54			330	375	4,000
GE145☐1887S	817			330	375	
GE146☐1888	133			330	375	4,000
GE147☐1888 0	21			330	375	
GE148☐1888S	649			330	375	
GE149☐1889	4	375	650	850	1,500	4,000
GE150☐1889S	425			330	375	
GE151☐1890	58			330	375	4,000
GE152☐1890CC	17	300	430	535	950	
GE153☐1891	92			330	375	4,000
GE154☐1891CC	104		310	355	525	
GE155☐1892	798			330	375	3,850
GE158☐1892CC	40		410	560	950	
GE156☐1892 0	29			330	500	
GE157☐1892S	115			330	375	
GE159☐1893	1,841			330	375	3,850
GE160☐1893 0	17		310	460	750	
GE162☐1893CC	14	450	600	950		
GE161☐1893S	141			330	375	
GE163☐1894	2,471			330	375	3,850
GE164☐1894 0	107			330	375	
GE165☐1894S	25			330	375	
GE166☐1895	568			330	375	3,850
GE167☐1895 0	98			330	375	
GE168☐1895 S	49			330	375	

See note on bottom of page 156.

DATE	Mintages in 1000's	A.D.P. AU	Unc.	Proof
GE169☐1896	76	330	375	3,850
GE170☐1896S	124	330	375	
GE171☐1897	1,000	330	375	3,850
GE172☐1897 O	42	330	375	
GE173☐1897S	235	330	375	
GE174☐1898	812	330	375	3,850
GE174☐1898S	474	330	375	
GE176☐1899	1,262	330	375	4,500
GE177☐1899 O	37	330	375	
GE178☐1899S	841	330	375	
GE179☐1900	294	330	375	4,000
GE180☐1900S	81	330	375	
GE181☐1901	1,719	330	375	3,850
GE182☐1901 O	72	330	375	
GE183☐1901S	2,813	330	375	
GE184☐1902	83	330	375	3,850
GE185☐1902S	469	330	375	
GE186☐1903	126	330	375	3,850
GE187☐1903 O	113	330	375	
GE188☐1903S	538	330	375	
GE189☐1904	162	330	375	3,850
GE190☐1904 O	109	330	395	
GE191☐1905	201	330	375	3,850
GE192☐1905S	369	330	375	

See note on bottom of page 156.

EAGLES ($10.00 Gold Pieces)
LIBERTY HEAD WITH CORONET 1906-1907
MOTTO OVER EAGLE

DATE	Mintages in 1000's	AU	Unc.	Proof
GE193☐1906	165	330	375	3,850
GE195☐1906D	981	330	375	
GE194☐1906 0	87	330	375	
GE196☐1906S	457	330	375	
GE197☐1907	1,204	330	375	3,850
GE198☐1907D	1,030	330	375	
GE199☐1907S	210	330	375	

EAGLES ($10.00 Gold Pieces) - INDIAN HEAD 1907-1933
Designed by Augustus St. Gaudens

1907-1933 With Motto

1907-1908 Without Motto

DATE	Mintages in 1000's	A.D.P. (EF)	Ex.Fine	AU	Unc.
GE203☐1907 No Periods	239	400	500	550	850
GE200☐1907 Wire Rim with Periods Before and After Motto	(500)*	2,000	3,000	4,000	8,000
GE202☐1907 Rolled Rim. Periods	(42)*	Rare			29,000
GE204☐1908 No Motto	33	400	550	625	1,450
GE205☐1908D No Motto	210	400	525	575	925

*Total mintage

163

EAGLES ($10.00 Gold Pieces) INDIAN HEAD 1908-1933
WITH MOTTO ON REVERSE

DATE	Mintages in 1000's	A.D.P. (EF)	Ex.Fine	AU	Unc.	Proof
GE206 □ 1908	341			500	625	6,275
GE207 □ 1908D	836			550	875	
GE208 □ 1908S	60	400	695	775	3,300	
GE209 □ 1909	185			500	625	6,275
GE210 □ 1909D	122			500	850	
GE211 □ 1909S	292			550	1,475	
GE212 □ 1910	319			500	625	6,275
GE213 □ 1910D	2,357			500	625	
GE214 □ 1910S	811			550	1,500	
GE215 □ 1911	506			500	625	6,275
GE216 □ 1911D	30	475	750	825	5,450	
GE217 □ 1911S	51	400	510	565	2,150	
GE218 □ 1912	405			500	625	6,275
GE219 □ 1912S	300	400	500	550	1,825	
GE220 □ 1913	442			500	625	6,275
GE221 □ 1913S	66	400	700	795	7,300	
GE222 □ 1914	151			500	625	6,275
GE223 □ 1914D	343			500	635	
GE224 □ 1914S	208			550	1,675	
GE225 □ 1915	351			500	625	6,275
GE226 □ 1915S	59	400	550	625	2,550	
GE227 □ 1916S	138	400	500	550	1,325	
GE228 □ 1920S	126	6,000	8,800	10,000	17,000	
GE229 □ 1926	1,014			500	600	
GE230 □ 1930S	96	3,000	5,000	7,500	12,650	
GE231 □ 1932	4,463			500	600	
GE232 □ 1933	312	10,000	15,000	25,000	49,500	

Please note: Unpriced Indian eagles are not considered numismatic items in less than AU condition, and generally bring about 250-300 each.

DOUBLE EAGLES ($20.00 Gold Pieces) 1849-1933

Designed by James Longacre, this is the heaviest U.S. coin, weight 516 grains, 900 fine. The government authorized its minting after gold was discovered in California

LIBERTY HEAD, NO MOTTO ON REVERSE 1849-1866

DATE	Mintages in 1000's	A.D.P. (VF)	V.Fine	Ex.Fine	AU	Unc.
GD1 ☐ 1849			UNIQUE - U.S. MINT COLLECTION			
GD2 ☐ 1850	1,170		600	660	810	1,850
GD3 ☐ 1850 0	141		690	850	1,150	3,750
GD4 ☐ 1851	2,087		600	660	810	1,495
GD5 ☐ 1851 0	315		630	840	1,150	3,300
GD6 ☐ 1852	2,053		600	660	810	1,495
GD8 ☐ 1852 0	190		630	815	1,150	3,250
GD10 ☐ 1853	1,261		600	660	810	1,495
GD11 ☐ 1853 0	71		655	950	1,800	3,750
GD12 ☐ 1854	758		605	660	810	1,495
GD14 ☐ 1854 0	3		1982 AUCTION AU		40,000	
GD15 ☐ 1854S	141		630	720	1,000	2,800
GD16 ☐ 1855	365		630	660	810	1,495
GD17 ☐ 1855 0	8	1,500	2,000	3,200	5,750	10,000
GD18 ☐ 1855S	880		600	660	810	1,495

Used $20 gold coins are generally worth only the daily ounce price for gold.

DOUBLE EAGLE ($2.00 Gold Pieces)
LIBERTY HEAD NO MOTTO ON REVERSE 1856-1866 (Cont'd.)

DATE	Mintages in 1000's	A.D.P. (VF)	V.Fine	Ex.Fine	AU	Unc.	Proof
GD19 ☐1856	330		600	660	810	1,495	
GD20 ☐1856 O	2		1982 AUCTION EF			45,000	
GD21 ☐1856S	1,190		600	660	810	1,495	
GD22 ☐1857	439		600	660	810	1,495	
GD23 ☐1857 O	30		700	900	1,400	4,000	
GD24 ☐1857S	970		600	660	810	1,495	
GD25 ☐1858	212		630	660	850	1,495	
GD26 ☐1858 O	35		825	1,400	2,250	4,000	
GD27 ☐1858S	847		600	660	810	1,495	
GD28 ☐1859	44		825	950	1,550	3,500	
GD29 ☐1859 O	9	1,700	2,500	3,000	4,250	7,250	
GD30 ☐1859S	636		600	660	810	1,495	
GD31 ☐1860	578		605	660	810	1,495	12,000
GD32 ☐1860 O	7	2,500	3,500	4,000	5,250	8,000	
GD33 ☐1860S	545		630	660	810	1,495	
GD34 ☐1861	2,976		600	660	810	1,495	10,500
GD36 ☐1861 O	18	1,000	1,500	2,250	3,750	7,500	
GD37 ☐1861S	768		630	660	810	1,495	
GD39 ☐1862	92		700	750	1,100	3,500	8,000
GD40 ☐1862S	854		630	660	810	1,495	
GD41 ☐1863	143		605	750	1,500	3,300	8,000
GD42 ☐1863S	967		600	660	810	1,495	
GD43 ☐1864	204		600	725	1,500	3,200	10,500
GD44 ☐1864S	794		630	660	810	1,495	
GD45 ☐1865	351		615	705	1,300	3,200	10,500
GD46 ☐1865S	1,042		600	660	810	1,495	
GD47 ☐1866S	842		690	1,200	1,850	4,000	

See note on bottom of page 165.

DOUBLE EAGLE ($20.00 Gold Pieces)
LIBERTY HEAD, WITH MOTTO AND "TWENTY D" 1866-1876

(Mint Mark is below Eagle on Reverse)

DATE	Mintages in 1000's	A.D.P. (EF)	Ex.Fine	AU	Unc.	Proof
GD48☐1866.	699		695	860	1.500	10.500
GD49☐1866S	842		695	860	1.500	
GD50☐1867.	251		640	725	950	10.500
GD51☐1867S	920		725	775	1.300	
GD52☐1868.	99		725	775	1.750	10.000
GD53☐1868S	837		695	775	1.350	
GD54☐1869.	175		725	775	1.100	10.500
GD55☐1869S	687		655	775	1.100	
GD56☐1870.	155		725	775	1.050	10.000
GD58☐1870CC		1982 AUCTION VF 20.000				
GD57☐1870S	982		655	775	1.050	
GD59☐1871.	80		655	775	1.500	8.000
GD61☐1871CC	17	1.700	2.750	3.200	4.000	
GD60☐1871S	928		655	775	950	
GD62☐1872.	252		655	775	950	8.000
GD64☐1872CC	27	900	1.450	2.400		
GD63☐1872S	780		665	750	900	

See note at bottom of page 165.

DOUBLE EAGLES ($20.00 Gold Pieces)
LIBERTY HEAD, WITH MOTTO ON REVERSE 1873-1876 (Cont'd.)

DATE	Mintages in 1000's	A.O.P. (EF)	Ex.Fine	AU	Unc.	Proof
GD66☐1873 Open 3	1,710			660	775	
GD65☐1873 Closed 3			725	775	1,750	7,000
GD69☐1873CC	22		1,200	1,750	2,800	
GD67☐1873S	1,041			660	775	
GD70☐1874	367			660	775	7,200
GD72☐1874CC	115			1,150	1,750	
GD71☐1874S	1,214			660	775	
GD73☐1875	296			660	775	52,500
GD75☐1875CC	111			750	1,225	
GD74☐1875S	1,230			660	775	
GD76☐1876	584			660	775	7,200
GD78☐1876CC	138			775	1,250	
GD77☐1876S	1597			660	775	

LIBERTY HEAD, WITH MOTTO & "TWENTY DOLLARS", 1877-1907

(Mint Mark is below Eagle in Reverse)

DOUBLE EAGLES ($20.00 Gold Pieces)
LIBERTY HEAD, WITH MOTTO & TWENTY DOLLARS 1877-1885

DATE	Mintages in 1000's	A.D.P. (EF)	Ex.Fine	AU	Unc.	Proof
GD79 ☐1877	398			620	675	7,200
GD81 ☐1877CC	43		800	900	1,950	
GD80 ☐1877S	1,735			620	675	
GD82 ☐1878	535			620	675	7,200
GD84 ☐1878CC	13		845	1,250	2,750	
GD83 ☐1878S	1,739			620	675	
GD85 ☐1879	208			620	675	7,200
GD88 ☐1879CC	11		870	2,200	3,750	
GD86 ☐1879 0	2	~1,350	2,500	4,750	8,000	
GD87 ☐1879S	1,224			620	675	
GD89 ☐1880	51			620	675	6,750
GD90 ☐1880S	836			620	675	
GD91 ☐1881	2	2,500	4,500	7,500	14,000	20,000
GD92 ☐1881S	727			620	675	
GD93 ☐1882	(630)*	8,000	15,000	23,500	35,000	20,000
GD95 ☐1882CC	39		740	850	1,450	
GD94 ☐1882S	1,125			620	675	
GD96 ☐1883	(92)*		1982 AUCTION PROOF			80,000
GD98 ☐1883CC	60		640	800	1,400	
GD97 ☐1883S	1,189			620	675	
GD99 ☐1884	(71*)		1982 AUCTION PROOF			80,000
GD101☐1884CC	81		665	800	1,400	
GD100☐1884S	916			620	675	
GD102☐1885	(828)*	4,000	7,500	13,000	25,000	27,500
GD104☐1885CC	9		1,050	1,700	3,000	
GD103☐1885S	683			620	675	

*Total Mintage

DATE	Mintages in 1000's	A.D.P. (EF)	Ex.Fine	AU	Unc.	Proof
GD105☐1886	1	5.000	9.400	13.500	22.000	20.000
GD106☐1887	(121)*	1982 AUCTION PROOF ONLY				42.500
GD107☐1887S	283			620	675	
GD108☐1888	226			620	675	6.250
GD109☐1888S	860			620	675	
GD110☐1889	44			620	675	5.775
GD112☐1889CC	31		870	1.050	1.450	
GD111☐1889S	775			620	675	
GD113☐1890	76			620	675	5.775
GD115☐1890CC	91			675	1.000	
GD114☐1890S	803			620	675	
GD116☐1891	1	2.000	3.000	4.250	7.500	8.000
GD118☐1891CC	5	1.000	1.750	2.800	5.500	
GD117☐1891S	1.288			620	675	
GD119☐1892	5		1.100	2.300	3.700	5.775
GD121☐1892CC	27		745	850	1.400	
GD120☐1892S	930			620	675	
GD122☐1893	344			620	675	5.775
GD124☐1893CC	18		720	825	1.300	
GD123☐1893S	996			620	675	
GD125☐1894	1.369			620	675	5.775
GD126☐1894S	1.049			620	675	
GD127☐1895	1.115			620	675	5.775
GD128☐1895S	1.143			620	675	
GD129☐1896	793			620	675	5.775

*Total mintage

DOUBLE EAGLES ($20.00 Gold Pieces)
LIBERTY HEAD WITH MOTTO AND "TWENTY DOLLARS"
1896-1907 (Cont'd.)

DATE	Mintages in 1000's	A.D.P. (Unc.)	Unc.	Proof
GD130☐1896S	1,404		675	
GD131☐1897	1,383		675	5.775
GD132☐1897S	1,470		675	
GD133☐1898	170		675	5.775
GD134☐1898S	2,575		675	
GD135☐1899	1,669		675	5.775
GD136☐1899S	2,010		675	
GD137☐1900	1,875		675	5.775
GD138☐1900S	2,459		675	
GD139☐1901	111		675	5.775
GD140☐1901S	1,596		675	
GD141☐1902	31		675	5.775
GD142☐1902S	1,754		675	
GD143☐1903	287		675	5.775
GD144☐1903S	954		675	
GD145☐1904	6,257		675	5.775
GD146☐1904S	5,134		675	
GD147☐1905	59		675	5.775
GD148☐1905S	1,813		675	
GD149☐1906	70		675	5.775
GD150☐1906D	620		675	
GD151☐1906S	2,066		675	
GD152☐1907	1,452		675	5.775
GD153☐1907D	842		675	
GD154☐1907S	2,166		675	

See note at bottom of page 165.

DOUBLE EAGLES ($20.00 Gold Pieces)

The $20 Standing Liberty type was designed by Augustus St. Gaudens at the behest of President Theodore Roosevelt who sought to raise the standards of our coinage as compared to European issues. The motto "In God We Trust" was left off by presidential request and reinstated by Congress in 1908, on both the $20 and $10 denominations.

LIBERTY STANDING — ST. GAUDENS
DATE IN ROMAN NUMERALS MCMVII

DATE	Mintages in 1000's	A.D.P.	AU	Unc.	Proof
GD155 ☐ MCMVII Extra High Relief Lettered Edge.......		1982 AUCTION			220,000
☐ MCMVII Extra High Relief Plain Edge..........		UNIQUE			
GD156 ☐ MCMVII Wire Rim..........	11,250	3,000	9,400	8,000	
☐ MCMVII Flat Rim..........		3,000	4,400	8,000	

DATE	Mintages in 100's	A.D.P. EF	Ex.Fine	AU	Unc.
GD157 ☐ 1907	362				745
GD158 ☐ 1908	4,272				745
GD159 ☐ 1908 D	664				745

LIBERTY STANDING — ST. GAUDENS
WITH MOTTO ON REVERSE 1908-1933

See note at bottom of page 165.

DOUBLE EAGLES ($20.00 Gold Pieces)
LIBERTY STANDING — ST. GAUDENS
WITH MOTTO ON REVERSE 1908-1922

DATE	Mintages in 1000's	A.D.P. [EF]	Ex.Fine	AU	Unc.	Proof
GD160□1908	156				765	11,650
GD161□1908D	349				765	
GD162□1908S	22		935	1,050	3,575	
GD163□1909	161				950	11,650
GD164□1909 9 over 8					915	
GD165□1909D	52			825	2,700	
GD166□1909S	2,775				745	
GD167□1910	482				745	11,650
GD168□1910D	429				745	
GD169□1910S	2,128				745	
GD170□1911	197				765	11,650
GD171□1911D	846				745	
GD172□1911S	776				745	
GD173□1912	150				765	11,650
GD174□1913	169				765	11,650
GD175□1913D	393				745	
GD176□1913S	34				1,075	
GD177□1914	95				800	11,650
GD178□1914D	453				745	
GD179□1914S	1,498				745	
GD180□1915	152				765	11,650
GD181□1915S	567				745	
GD182□1916S	769				745	
GD183□1920	228				765	
GD184□1920S	558	5,000	8,250	11,000	17,000	
GD185□1921	528	6,000	10,725	15,000	22,000	
GD186□1922	1,375				715	

See note at bottom of page 165.

DATE	Mintages in 1000's	A.D.P. (EF)	Ex.Fine	AU	Unc.
GD187 ☐ 1922S	2,658			840	1,050
GD188 ☐ 1923	566				715
GD189 ☐ 1923D	1,702				760
GD190 ☐ 1924	4,232				715
GD191 ☐ 1924D	3,049			1,225	2,100
GD192 ☐ 1924S	2,927			1,175	2,025
GD193 ☐ 1925	2,832				715
GD194 ☐ 1925D	2,938			1,325	2,200
GD195 ☐ 1925S	3,776			1,225	2,400
GD196 ☐ 1926	817				715
GD197 ☐ 1926D	481			1,300	2,550
GD198 ☐ 1926S	2,041			1,100	1,800
GD199 ☐ 1927	2,947				715
GD200 ☐ 1927D	180		Private Sale 1983		250,000
GD201 ☐ 1927S	3,107	2,000	3,300	4,500	8,750
GD202 ☐ 1928	8,816				715
GD203 ☐ 1929	1,780	2,000	4,400	4,900	7,250
GD204 ☐ 1930S	74	4,500	7,700	8,750	15,000
GD205 ☐ 1931	2,938	4,000	7,000	8,000	12,500
GD206 ☐ 1931D	106	4,000	7,250	8,500	15,000
GD207 ☐ 1932	1,102	5,000	8,400	9,850	16,500
GD208 ☐ 1933	446		Not Legal To Own		

See note at bottom of page 165.

U.S. SILVER COMMEMORATIVE COINAGE

It has been said that the world's first commemorative coin was a tetradrachm issued by Philip II of Macedon, father of Alexander the Great about 350BC, in honor of his horse which had won an Olympic race. Since that time virtually all nations have minted coins commemorating various important events and people. Our first commemorative coin was the half dollar put out for the World Columbian Exposition in Chicago in 1892-93, at which time our only commemorative quarter, the Isabella quarter, was also issued. These were followed, in 1900 by a silver dollar honoring Lafayette, the only such we have minted. Since then we have minted 141 other half dollars, nine $1 gold coins, two $2.50 gold coins and two $50 gold coins, all commemorating some historical event.

As a general rule, commemorative coins tend to be rather crowded as to subject matter apparently it having been the intent of the various designers to immortalize as much as possible. In addition, these pieces were generally struck at odd times during the day when the mint was not occupied with usual business. Consequently, the series is not noted for clarity of strike. Also, most were jealously hoarded by their owners so that uncirculated pieces form the bulk of the coins available today. This series is not usually collected in less than uncirculated condition.

Medals are not in the same category as commemorative coins, as the medal is not a medium of exchange (as a coin is) and its only value is its metallic content, or as an item for a collector of medals.

The Unc. prices listed in this section are for coins which have no wear (MS-60). However, such coins will possess — in most cases — handling marks, and will have little or no original luster remaining on the coin's surfaces. Thus, superior specimens will be worth more than the noted values.

The Isabella quarter was authorized by The Board of Lady Managers of the Columbian Exposition on March 3, 1893. It was designed by Charles E. Barber, whose work may be seen on many other American coins.

DATE	Mintages in Full	A.D.P.	Unc.
CH1 ☐1893 Isabella	24,214	250	450

LAFAYETTE DOLLAR

Obverse shows Washington and Lafayette in profile, reverse being equestrian statue of Lafayette.

CH144☐1900 Lafayette	36,026	500	850

COLUMBIAN
EXPOSITION
HALF DOLLAR

1892-1893

DATE	Mintages in Full	A.D.P.	Unc.
CH2 ☐ 1892 Columbian	950,000	12	25
CH3 ☐ 1893 Columbian	1,550,405	12	25

CH4 ☐ 1915S Pan Pacific Exposition	27,134	250	450

DATE	Mintages in Full	A.D.P.	Unc.
CH5 ☐ 1918 Illinois Centennial	100,058	50	95

	Mintages in Full	A.D.P.	Unc.
CH6 ☐ 1920 Maine Centennial	50,028	65	110

	Mintages in Full	A.D.P.	Unc.
CH7 ☐ 1920 Pilgrim Tercentennial	152,112	35	60
CH8 ☐ 1921 Pilgrim Tercentennial	20,053	100	165

DATE	Mintages in Full	A.D.P.	Unc.
CH9 ☐1921 Missouri Centennial	15,428	300	500
CH10☐1921 Same w/2x4 on Obverse *	5,000	325	550

| CH11☐1921 Alabama Centennial .... | 59,038 | 160 | 275 |
| CH12☐1921 Same w/2x2 on Obverse .... | 6,006 | 210 | 375 |

| CH13☐1922 Grant Memorial .... | 67,405 | 60 | 100 |
| CH14☐1922 Same w/Star on Obverse * .... | 4,256 | 375 | 650 |

* Beware of Counterfeits

SILVER COMMEMORATIVES (Cont'd.)

DATE	Mintages in Full	A.D.P.	Unc.
CH15☐1923S Monroe Doctrine 274,077		30	55

CH16☐1924 Huguenot Walloon. 142,080		60	110

CH17☐1925 Lexington-Concord 162,013		30	60

DATE	Mintages in Full	A.D.P.	Unc.
CH18☐1925 Stone Mountain	1,315,709	25	45

CH19☐1925S California Diamond Jubilee	87,594	70	125

CH20☐1925S Fort Vancouver	14,944	250	450

DATE	Mintages in Full	A.D.P.	Unc.
CH21☐1926 Sesquicentennial	141.120	30	50

CH22☐1926 Oregon Trail	48,955	65	110
CH23☐1926S Oregon Trail	83,055	65	110
CH24☐1928 Oregon Trail	6,028	140	235
CH25☐1933D Oregon Trail	5,008	260	450
CH26☐1934D Oregon Trail	7,006	110	180
CH27☐1936 Oregon Trail	10,006	90	150
CH28☐1936S Oregon Trail	5,006	140	225
CH29☐1937D Oregon Trail	12,008	80	130
CH30☐1938 Oregon Trail	6,006	100	170
CH32☐1938D Oregon Trail	6,005	100	170
CH31☐1938S Oregon Trail	6,006	100	170
CH33☐1939 Oregon Trail	3,004	150	245
CH35☐1939D Oregon Trail	3,004	150	245
CH34☐1939S Oregon Trail	3,005	150	245

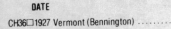

DATE	Mintages in Full	A.D.P.	Unc.
CH36☐1927 Vermont (Bennington)	28,162	130	235

CH37☐1928 Hawaii Sesquicentennial.............	10,000	450	850

CH38☐1934 Maryland Tercentennial...............	25,015	80	135

DATE	Mintages in Full	A.D.P.	Unc.
CH39☐1934 Texas Centennial	61,413	70	120
CH40☐1935 Texas Centennial	9,996	60	115
CH42☐1935D Texas Centennial	10,007	60	115
CH41☐1935S Texas Centennial	10,008	60	115
CH43☐1936 Texas Centennial	8,911	60	115
CH45☐1936D Texas Centennial	9,039	60	115
CH44☐1936S Texas Centennial	9,055	60	115
CH46☐1937 Texas Centennial	6,571	80	150
CH48☐1937D Texas Centennial	6,605	80	125
CH47☐1937S Texas Centennial	6,637	80	125
CH49☐1938 Texas Centennial	3,780	100	175
CH51☐1938D Texas Centennial	3,775	100	175
CH50☐1938S Texas Centennial	3,814	100	175

CH52☐1934 Boone Bi-Centennial	10,007	80	125
CH53☐1935 Boone Bi-Centennial	10,010	50	75
CH54☐1935D Boone Bi-Centennial	5,005	80	125
CH55☐1935S Boone Bi-Centennial	5,005	80	125
CH56☐1935 Boone Bi-Cent. Sm. 1934 Rev.	10,008	100	200
CH57☐1935D Boone Bi-Centennial Sm. 1934 Rev.	2,003	250	400
CH58☐1935S Boone Bi-Centennial Sm. 1934 Rev.	2,004	250	400
CH59☐1936 Boone Bi-Centennial	12,012	50	75
CH60☐1936D Boone Bi-Centennial	5,005	80	125

SILVER COMMEMORATIVES (Cont'd.)

DATE	Mintages in Full	A.D.P.	Unc.
CH61☐1936S Boone Bi-Centennial	5,006	80	125
CH62☐1937 Boone Bi-Centennial	9,810	80	175
CH63☐1937D Boone Bi-Centennial	2,506	275	425
CH64☐1937S Boone Bi-Centennial	2,506	275	425
CH65☐1938 Boone Bi-Centennial	2,100	225	350
CH66☐1938D Boone Bi-Centennial	2,100	225	350
CH67☐1938S Boone Bi-Centennial	2,100	225	350

	Mintages in Full	A.D.P.	Unc.
CH69☐1935 Arkansas Centennial	13,012	50	80
CH70☐1935D Arkansas Centennial	5,505	80	120
CH71☐1935S Arkansas Centennial	5,506	80	120
CH72☐1936 Arkansas Centennial	9,660	55	90
CH73☐1936D Arkansas Centennial	9,660	55	90
CH74☐1936S Arkansas Centennial	9,662	55	90
CH75☐1937 Arkansas Centennial	5,505	60	95
CH76☐1937D Arkansas Centennial	5,505	60	95
CH77☐1937S Arkansas Centennial	5,506	60	95
CH78☐1938 Arkansas Centennial	3,156	100	165
CH79☐1938D Arkansas Centennial	3,155	100	165
CH80☐1938S Arkansas Centennial	3,156	100	165
CH81☐1939 Arkansas Centennial	2,104	200	325
CH82☐1939D Arkansas Centennial	2,104	200	325
CH83☐1939S Arkansas Centennial	2,105	200	325

SILVER COMMEMORATIVES (Cont'd.)

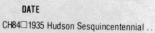

DATE	Mintages in Full	A.D.P.	Unc.
CH84☐1935 Hudson Sesquincentennial	10,008	350	525

CH85☐1935S San Diego Exposition	70,132	50	85
CH86☐1936D San Diego Exposition	30,082	70	110

CH87☐1935 Old Spanish Trail	10,008	450	700

DATE	Mintages in Full	A.D.P.	Unc.
CH88☐1936 Rhode Island	20,013	75	120
CH89☐1936D Rhode Island	15,010	80	125
CH90☐1936S Rhode Island	15,011	80	125

| CH91☐1936 Cleveland Exposition | 50,030 | 60 | 85 |

| CH92☐1936 Wisconsin | 25,015 | 140 | 225 |

DATE	Mintages in Full	A.D.P.	Unc.
CH93□1936 Cinc. Music Center	5,005	175	300
CH94□1936D Cinc. Music Center	5,005	175	300
CH95□1936S Cinc. Music Center	5,005	175	300

CH96□1936 Long Island	81,826	45	75

CH97□1936 York County Maine	25,015	135	210

DATE	Mintages in Full	A.D.P.	Unc.
CH98 ☐1936 Bridgeport. Conn.	25,015	100	150

| CH99 ☐1936 Lynchburg. Va..................... | 20,013 | 120 | 185 |

| CH101☐1936 Elgin .... | 20,015 | 115 | 175 |

DATE	Mintages in Full	A.D.P.	Unc.
CH100☐1936 Albany	16,671	160	240

CH102☐1936S Oakland Bay Bridge	71,424	70	105

CH103☐1936 Columbia, S.C.	9,007	150	250
CH104☐1936D Columbia, S.C.	8,009	150	250
CH105☐1936S Columbia, S.C.	8,007	150	250

	Mintages		
DATE	in Full	A.D.P.	Unc.
CH106□1936 Arkansas (Robinson)	25,262	80	120

| CH107□1936 Delaware Tercentennial.............. | 20,993 | 140 | 210 |

| CH108□1936 Battle of Gettysburg .... | 26,630 | 170 | 245 |

DATE	Mintages in Full	A.D.P.	Unc.
CH109☐1936 Norfolk Va.	16,936	225	340

| CH110☐1937 Roanoke Island N.C. .... | 29,030 | 100 | 170 |

| CH111☐1937 Battle of Antietam .... | 18,023 | 200 | 310 |

SILVER COMMEMORATIVES (Cont'd.)

	DATE	Mintages in Full	A.D.P.	Unc.
CH112☐	1938 New Rochelle N.Y.	15,226	240	350

	DATE	Mintages in Full	A.D.P.	Unc.
CH113☐	1946 Iowa Centennial	100,057	55	85

	DATE	Mintages in Full	A.D.P.	Unc.
CH114☐	1946 B.T. Washington	1,000,546	8	14
CH115☐	1946D B.T. Washington	200,113	10	18

DATE	Mintages in Full	A.D.P.	Unc.
CH116☐1946S B.T. Washington	400,279	10	17
CH117☐1947 B.T. Washington	100,017	15	24
CH118☐1947D B.T. Washington	100,017	15	24
CH119☐1947S B.T. Washington	100,017	15	24
CH120☐1948 B.T. Washington	8,005	30	50
CH121☐1948D B.T. Washington	8,005	30	50
CH122☐1948S B.T. Washington	8,005	30	50
CH123☐1949 B.T. Washington	6,004	40	70
CH124☐1949D B.T. Washington	6,004	40	70
CH125☐1949S B.T. Washington	6,004	40	70
CH126☐1950 B.T. Washington	6,004	50	80
CH127☐1950D B.T. Washington	6,004	50	80
CH128☐1950S B.T. Washington	512,091	10	18
CH129☐1951 B.T. Washington	510,082	10	16
CH130☐1951D B.T. Washington	7,004	30	50
CH131☐1951S B.T. Washington	7,004	30	50

WASHINGTON-CARVER

DATE	Mintages in Full	A.D.P.	Unc.
CH132☐1951 Washington Carver	110,018	9	18
CH133☐1951D Washington Carver	10,004	20	40
CH134☐1951S Washington Carver	10,004	20	40
CH135☐1952 Washington Carver	2,006,292	8	14
CH136☐1952D Washington Carver	8,006	40	60
CH137☐1952S Washington Carver	8,006	40	60
CH138☐1953 Washington Carver	8,003	45	75
CH139☐1953D Washington Carver	8,003	45	75
CH140☐1953S Washington Carver	108,020	9	18
CH141☐1954 Washington Carver	12,006	25	45
CH142☐1954D Washington Carver	12,006	25	45
CH143☐1954D Washington Carver	122,024	9	18

U.S. PROOF SETS — 1936 — TO DATE

Proof coins were first struck in the early 1830's, and have been minted with some degree of irregularity ever since. In the beginning they were intended to show Congress what the upcoming year's coins would look like, which accounts for the small odd amounts issued. (In some cases, the number of proofs corresponds to the number of members in these early years). Because they were perfect coins, they were in demand by collectors, and gradually the numbers were increased to accommodate the influential. In 1936, the Philadelphia mint struck the first proof set for general distribution, continuing until 1942, when wartime pressures on the mint forced discontinuance. (The mint at this time was striking coins for many foreign governments and colonies which had lost their parent mints in Europe). In 1950, proof sets were again minted in Philadelphia and have continued yearly to date with the exception of 1965-7 when the sandwich coins came into being. In 1968, true proof sets were struck again, this time at the San Francisco mint, where they are still made. These all bear the "S" mint mark, the only US proofs which are so marked with the exception of the 1942 nickels.

U.S. PROOF SETS - 1936 TO DATE

DATE	Mintages in Full	A.D.P.	Proof Set	DATE	Mintages in Full	A.D.P.	Proof Set
☐1936	3,837	3,000	5,000	☐1963	3,075,645	12	20
☐1937	5,542	2,000	3,200	☐1964	3,949,634	11	20
☐1938	8,045	1,000	1,800	☐1965 SMS	2,360,000	3	5
☐1939	8,795	900	1,400	☐1966 SMS	2,201,583	3.50	5
☐1940	11,246	700	1,200	☐1967 SMS	1,863,344	8	13
☐1941	15,287	600	1,000	☐1968S*		6,000	10,000
☐1942 One Nickel	21,120	600	1,000	☐1968S	3,041,508	4	6
☐1942 Two Nickel		800	1,800	☐1969S	2,934,600	4	6
☐1950	51,386	350	750	☐1970S	2,632,810	7	12
☐1951	57,500	225	375	☐1970S small 7		80	125
☐1952	81,980	125	200	☐1970S*		600	900
☐1953	128,800	90	140	☐1971S	3,224,138	3	5
☐1954	233,300	50	80	☐1971S*		700	1,200
☐1955 Box		45	70	☐1972S	3,267,667	3	6
☐1955 Flat Pack	378,200	48	75	☐1973S	2,769,624	6	9
☐1956	699,384	20	35	☐1974S	2,617,350	6	9.50
☐1957	1,247,952	13	22	☐1975S	2,845,450	8	14
☐1958	875,652	19	27	☐1976S (3 pc. 40%)	1,045,412	10	16
				☐1976S	4,149,730	5	9
☐1959	1,149,291	16	24	☐1976S (Bicentennial Unc. Sets)	1,398,200	7	11
☐1960 Small Date	1,691,602	25	38				
☐1960 Large Date		12	20	☐1977S	3,251,152	4.50	7.50
☐1961	3,028,244	12	20	☐1978S	3,127,781	7	11
☐1962	3,218,019	12	20	☐1979S	3,677,175	12	11
				☐1979S Type 2 ...		100	165
				☐1980S	3,554,806	6	10
				☐1981S	4,063,083	7	11
				☐1981S Type 2 ...		130	200
				☐1982S		12	19

*1968 and 1970. dime without "S". 1971. nickel without "S".

GOLD COMMEMORATIVES

DATE	Mintages in Full	A.D.P. (AU)	AU	Unc.
GC1 ☐1903 La. Purchase/Jefferson	17,500	250	395	775
GC2 ☐1903 La. Purchase/McKinley	17,500	250	395	775
GC3 ☐1904 Lewis & Clark	10,025	350	550	1,300
GC4 ☐1905 Lewis & Clark	10,041	350	550	1,300
GC5 ☐1915S Pan-Pacific $1.00	15,000	200	350	800

GOLD COMMEMORATIVES

DATE	Mintages in Full	A.D.P. (AU)	AU	Unc.
GC6 ☐ 1915S Pan-Pacific $2.50	6,749	450	750	2,200

	Mintages in Full	A.D.P. (AU)	AU	Unc.
GC7 ☐ 1916 McKinley	15,000	225	350	775
GC8 ☐ 1917 McKinley	6,749	240	375	850

DATE	Mintages in Full	A.D.P. (AU)	AU	Unc.
GC9 ☐1922 Grant	9,997	375	625	1,200
GC10☐1922 Grant with star	10,000	400	650	1,300

DATE	Mintages in Full	A.D.P. (AU)	AU	Unc.
GC11☐1926 Sesquicentennial $2.50	46,019	200	325	500

DATE	Mintages in Full	A.D.P. (AU)	AU	Unc.
GC12☐1915S Pan-Pacific $50 Round	483	14,000	20,000	35,000

DATE	Mintages in Full	A.D.P. (AU)	AU	Unc.
GC13☐1915S Pan-Pacific $50 Octagonal	645	10,000	16,000	25,000

Catalogue No.	Good	V.Good	Fine	V.Fine	Ex.Fine	Unc.	Proof		Cost	Value

Catalogue No.	Good	V.Good	Fine	V.Fine	Ex.Fine	Unc.	Proof		Cost	Value

Catalogue No.	Good	V.Good	Fine	V.Fine	Ex.Fine	Unc.	Proof		Cost	Value

Catalogue No.	Good	V.Good	Fine	V.Fine	Ex.Fine	Unc.	Proof		Cost	Value

Catalogue No.	Good	V.Good	Fine	V.Fine	Ex.Fine	Unc.	Proof		Cost	Value